CONTENTS

INTRODUCTION

100 Literacy Homework Activities: Year 1

About the series

The *100 Literacy Homework Activities* series provides easy-to-use, photocopiable homework sheets for Key Stage 1 and 2 children. Each book in the series contains 100 homework activities that can be embedded into any school homework programme. Each activity sheet provides instructions for the child and a brief note to the helper, stating simply and clearly its purpose and suggesting support and/or further challenge to offer the child. The activities are clearly linked to the renewed Primary Framework for Literacy and are organised by Block (Narrative, Non-fiction, Poetry), then by Unit.

Core skills activities

At the end of each Unit, you will find a number of 'Core skills' activities, designed to support the development of key literacy skills such as word recognition (Years 1 and 2 only), word structure and spelling, and sentence structure and punctuation. Some of the Core skills activities are linked to the content of the Units; others are intended to be used for discrete teaching and can be used at any time.

Teachers' notes

The teachers' notes starting on page 8 provide further information about each activity, with notes on setting the homework, differentiation and follow-up work. The Narrative, Non-fiction and Poetry objectives on the teachers' notes show how activities are linked to the Unit plans, while the reference grid on pages 6 and 7 shows how the objectives from Strands 1 to 12 of the Framework are covered in the book. Links to the Scottish curriculum are provided on the Scholastic website (see page 7).

Using the resources

The best way to use these homework resources is to use them flexibly, integrating them with a series of literacy sessions over a number of days. At primary level, homework should be about 'consolidating and reinforcing skills and understanding, particularly in literacy and numeracy' (Department for Children, Schools and Families: Homework Guidelines). Although the homework sheets can be used to support assessment, their main purpose is to reinforce and extend literacy work carried out in class or to help children prepare for upcoming work.

Supporting your helpers

It is vital that parents or carers understand what you are trying to achieve with homework. As well as the 'Dear helper' notes on each sheet, there is a homework diary on page 5 which can be photocopied and sent home with the homework. Multiple copies of these can be fastened together to make a longer term homework record. Discuss with parents/carers what is meant by 'help'. Legitimate help will include sharing the reading of texts, helping to clarify problems, discussing possible answers and so on, but at some stage the child should be left to do his or her best. Tell parents/carers how much time you expect the child to spend on homework. If, after that time, a child is stuck, or has not finished, they should not be forced to continue. Ask parents/carers to write a brief explanation and say that you will give extra help the next day. If children are succeeding with a task and need more time, this can be allowed – but bear in mind that children need a varied and balanced home life!

Using the activities with *100 Literacy Framework Lessons*

Links have been provided on the teachers' notes for those who wish to use the homework activities with the corresponding *100 Literacy Framework Lessons* book. The teachers' notes show if and where a homework task might fit within the context of the appropriate *100 Literacy Framework Lessons* Unit.

Homework diary

Name of activity and date sent home	Helper's comments	Child's comments		Teacher's comments
		Did you like this? Draw a face. ☺ a lot ☺ a little ☹ not much	**How much did you learn?** Draw a face. ☺ a lot ☺ a little ☹ not much	

Framework objectives

Objectives	Supporting activities (page numbers)
Strand 1: Speaking	
Retell stories, ordering events using story language.	33, 40, 51, 53, 54, 56, 57, 58, 69
Tell stories and describe incidents from their own experience in an audible voice.	31, 32, 33, 41, 52, 65, 75
Interpret a text by reading aloud with some variety in pace and emphasis.	39, 51, 55
Experiment with and build new stores of words to communicate in different contexts.	111
Strand 2: Listening and responding	
Listen with sustained concentration, building new stores of words in different contexts.	53, 29, 69, 126
Listen to and follow instructions accurately, asking for help and clarification if necessary.	80
Strand 3: Group discussion and interaction	
Take turns to speak, listen to each other's suggestions and talk about what they are going to do.	29, 33
Ask and answer questions, make relevant contributions, offer suggestions and take turns.	68
Strand 4: Drama	
Explore familiar themes and characters through improvisation and role-play.	31, 33, 52, 54
Act out their own and well-known stories, using voices for characters.	51, 53, 54, 55, 58
Strand 5: Word recognition	
Recognise and use alternative ways of pronouncing the graphemes already taught.	49, 62, 103, 104
Recognise and use alternative ways of spelling the phonemes already taught and begin to know which words contain which spelling alternatives.	64, 73, 110, 114, 115, 126
Identify the constituent parts of two-syllable and three-syllable words to support the application of phonic knowledge and skills.	76
Recognise automatically an increasing number of familiar high frequency words.	47, 118
Apply phonic knowledge and skills as the prime approach to reading and spelling unfamiliar words that are not completely decodable.	42, 43, 76, 109
Read and spell phonically decodable two-syllable and three-syllable words.	88, 122
Strand 6: Word structure and spelling	
Spell new words using phonics as the prime approach.	63, 72, 73, 74, 83, 84, 90, 103, 104, 121, 122
Segment sounds into their constituent phonemes in order to spell them correctly.	38, 48, 63, 72, 122
Read and spell phonically decodable two-syllable and three-syllable words.	74

📖 SCHOLASTIC
www.scholastic.co.uk

Objectives	Supporting activities (page numbers)
Strand 6: Word structure and spelling (cont.)	
Children move from spelling simple CVC words to longer words that include common digraphs and adjacent consonants such as *brush*, *crunch*.	35, 38, 48, 72
Recognise and use alternative ways of spelling the graphemes already taught and begin to know which words contain which spelling alternatives.	64, 73, 116, 117, 118, 119, 120, 126, 127
Strand 7: Understanding and interpreting texts	
Identify the main events and characters in stories, and find specific information in simple texts.	28, 29, 30, 34, 36, 41, 45, 51, 52, 56, 65, 70, 85, 94, 95, 96, 97
Use syntax and context when reading for meaning.	60, 79, 85, 91, 94, 105, 117, 118
Make predictions showing an understanding of ideas, events and characters.	30, 65, 66, 67
Recognise the main elements that shape different texts.	50, 51, 71, 79, 80, 88, 89, 100, 105, 106, 107
Explore the effect of patterns of language and repeated words and phrases.	47, 116, 117, 123, 124
Strand 8: Engaging and responding to texts	
Select books for personal reading and give reasons for choices.	66
Visualise and comment on events, characters and ideas, making imaginative links to their own experiences.	56, 57, 66
Distinguish fiction and non-fiction texts and the different purposes for reading them.	79, 80, 94, 97
Strand 9: Creating and shaping texts	
Independently choose what to write about, plan and follow it through.	32, 93, 112, 113
Use key features of narrative in their own writing.	44
Convey information and ideas in simple non-narrative forms.	32, 41, 76, 77, 81, 86, 87, 98, 108, 112, 113, 124
Find and use new and interesting words and phrases, including story language.	45, 93, 111, 112, 113, 124
Create short simple texts on paper and screen that combine words with images (and sounds).	43, 59, 93, 98, 99, 106, 107
Strand 10: Text structure and organisation	
Write chronological and non-chronological texts using simple structures.	57, 59, 86, 87, 98, 99
Group written sentences together in chunks of meaning or subject.	57, 59, 100
Strand 11: Sentence structure and punctuation	
Compose and write simple sentences independently to communicate meaning.	34, 35, 36, 57, 59, 64, 73, 75, 77, 81, 82, 89, 92, 98, 99, 101, 108
Use capital letters and full stops when punctuating simple sentences.	34, 35, 36, 37, 46, 61, 64, 73, 75, 77, 78, 82, 89, 91, 92, 101, 102, 125

Links to the Scottish curriculum can be found at www.scholastic.co.uk/literacyhomework/y1 (click on Free resources)

Narrative – Unit 1 Stories with familiar settings

Page 28 Identify the characters
Narrative objective: To identify characters in a story using evidence from the text.
Setting the homework: Children will need to have read *Amazing Grace* by Mary Hoffman for this activity. Remind the children of the story and explain that they are going to identify characters in extracts from the story.
Differentiation: Some children may need help in reading the extracts. Ask the helper to support their child by reading with expression.
Back at school: Organise the children into pairs so that they can tell one another which characters are in the extracts. Use enlarged versions of the extracts for shared reading to establish the character in the extract.
Link to *100 Literacy Framework Lessons Y1:* NU1, Sequence 2, Phases 1 and 2: work on characters and the story of *Amazing Grace*.

Page 29 Identify the settings
Narrative objective: To identify settings in stories using evidence from texts.
Setting the homework: Children will need to have read *Amazing Grace* by Mary Hoffman for this activity. Explain that they are going to identify settings from extracts from the story. Point out the layout of the homework sheet each extract is followed by two questions.
Differentiation: Some children may need help in reading the extracts. Ask the helper to support their child by reading the extracts with expression.
Back at school: Talk about the importance of settings in a story and how these can affect a character's behaviour.
Link to *100 Literacy Framework Lessons Y1:* NU1, Sequence 2, Phase 2: work on the story of *Amazing Grace*.

Page 30 Describing characters
Narrative objective: To identify and visualise characters.
Setting the homework: Explain to the children that they will need their helper to help them to read the descriptions of the two characters. Demonstrate what to do by reading one of the extracts, discussing words that you might use to describe the character.
Differentiation: All children should attempt to draw a picture of the characters from listening to the descriptions. Ask helpers to support children in finding words to describe the characters by referring to the text on the sheet.
Back at school: Choose two children to share their pictures and words to describe the characters. As an additional activity collect all the words and ask groups of children to sort them on the basis of *most popular*, *popular* and *rare* in order to provide a word bank.
Link to *100 Literacy Framework Lessons Y1:* NU1, Sequence 1, Phase 1: work on characters.

Page 31 Story puppets
Narrative objective: To re-enact stories using puppets.
Setting the homework: Make clear the link between the homework and classroom activities for this Unit. Draw their attention to characterisation and why it is important to be able to describe the characters in stories. You will probably need to supply lollipop sticks or similar for the puppets.
Differentiation: Most children will be able to invent characters for telling a story. Some will need more help in providing descriptions of their characters.
Back at school: Choose a child to tell their story and another to describe a character in their story. Choose a child to give reasons for choosing the characters.

Page 32 Tell a story, write a story

Narrative objective: To tell a story based on own experience and compose a short written version.

Setting the homework: Discuss the picture on the homework sheet with the children and establish clearly for them the setting in which they are to base their stories.

Differentiation: All children should be encouraged to talk about their own experiences in the playground. Ask their helpers to provide support in terms of questions that will extend discussion and help create a focus for a piece of writing.

Back at school: Organise the children into groups so that they can share their stories. Choose some children to read their stories to the class.

Page 33 What's the story?

Narrative objective: To identify characters and events in a story and write own version.

Setting the homework: Tell the children that they are going to write a story using the picture on the sheet to help them. Ask them to think about who the characters in the story are and the main events. Explain that it is alright for their helper to write some of the story for them in the same way you do in class.

Back at school: Provide an opportunity for children to read some of the stories and use appropriate ones for the whole-class shared writing sessions in order to extend the teaching of story structures.

**Link to *100 Literacy Framework Lessons Y1:* **NU1, Sequence 1, Phase 1: work on characters.

Page 34 Draw a picture, write a sentence – Core skills

Objective: To compose and write simple sentences.

Setting the homework: Children will need to have read *Amazing Grace* by Mary Hoffman for this activity. Explain to the children that they are going to draw pictures and write sentences just as it says in the title of the homework sheet. Point out that the beginnings of the sentences have already been written to help them.

Differentiation: All the children should be able to draw the pictures. Most will require help to complete the sentences and some may need the helper to describe the sentences.

Back at school: Choose a child to show the first picture to the class and the corresponding picture in the book *Amazing Grace*. Choose another child to read aloud the second sentence and after hearing it choose another child to find the corresponding place in the book.

Page 35 Sh, sh, sh! – Core skills

Objective: To spell words that include common digraphs.

Setting the homework: Explain that the children are going to use the /sh/ sound to complete the spelling of words which they should then read and use to make sentences.

Differentiation: Some children could make sentences for all the words, whereas other children might make fewer sentences, using only familiar words from the list. The children can use the back of their sheet to write more sentences.

Back at school: In guided reading sessions, check that children are using phonic/graphic knowledge to help them decode unfamiliar words containing the 'sh' sound and spelling.

Page 36 Jumbled words – Core skills

Objective: To use capital letters and full stops when punctuating simple sentences.

Setting the homework: Tell the children to spend time with their helper discussing the picture before attempting the jumbled sentences. Remind the children to use the capital letters to help them find the beginning of a sentence and full stops to help them find the end.

Differentiation: Some children will need extra help when reading the words in the jumbled sentences.

Back at school: Ask some children to discuss the picture, intervening where necessary. Ask some children to think of other sentences they could compose from the picture, which they should write on a flipchart for all the others to see.

Page 37 Spot the stops! – Core skills

Objective: To use capital letters and full stops when punctuating simple sentences.
Setting the homework: Explain to the children that they should read the extract and put a ring round the full stops.
Differentiation: Some children will need support from their helper to read the text.
Back at school: Ask selected children to read out sentences they have written.

Page 38 Letter sounds – Core skills

Objective: To segment sounds into their constituent phonemes in order to spell them correctly.
Setting the homework: Remind the children about listening for the sounds of letters in words and tell them they are going to find the sounds in the list of words on the sheet by drawing a line between each sound. They should say each phoneme and demonstrate they can blend the sounds together.
Differentiation: Greater assistance will be required for children whose phonological awareness is less developed.
Back at school: Ask one or two children to demonstrate segmenting words by phonemes, then blending the phonemes together into words.

Narrative – Unit 2 Stories from a range of cultures/with predictable patterned language

Page 39 Mr. Bear
Narrative objective: To recite parts of stories and to read with expression.
Setting the homework: Explain to the children that they should read the extract with their helper to make it sound like Mr. Bear is really cross.
Differentiation: Some children will need to have their helper read the extract with them, joining in where possible.
Back at school: Select one or two children to read the extract to the class.

Page 40 Peace at Last
Narrative objective: To retell a story with a repeating phrase.
Setting the homework: Explain to the children that they should use the pictures and the repeating phrase to retell the story *Peace at Last*.
Differentiation: For less confident learners, ask the helper to read the story summary through several times to support their child's memory of the sequence.
Back at school: Display an enlarged version of the repeated phrase *"Oh, NO!" said Mr. Bear, "I can't stand THIS."* Ask a child to summarise the story using the pictures from the homework sheet while another child uses a pointer to point to the words of the repeating phrase as they are read by the whole class.

Page 41 Name the story
Narrative objective: To explore patterns in familiar stories.
Setting the homework: Discuss with the children some repeating lines in stories they might know. Tell the children that they can ask their helper to tell them some traditional tales or watch 'The Three Billy Goats Gruff' on the website given in the helper notes.
Back at school: Select a child to tell the class their favourite repeating lines from a story. Can the other children guess what the story is? Do this for several children and encourage them to draw upon wider reading and knowledge of stories.
Link to *100 Literacy Framework Lessons Y1:* NU2, Sequence 1, Phase 1: exploring repeating phrases in stories.

Page 42 Crazy animals
Narrative objective: To use language play.
Setting the homework: If the children have read the story *The Other Ark*, remind them of the story and the invented animals. Tell the children they are going to invent some new animals by making a special 'half and half' book. Ask the helpers to develop the discussion with their child by asking what the new creatures might look like, what they might eat, where they might live and how they might behave.
Back at school: Organise the children in pairs and using their 'half and half' books ask each of the children to take turns to create a new animal and to tell their partner all about it.
Link to *100 Literacy Framework Lessons Y1:* NU2, Sequence 2: work on the story of *The Other Ark*.

Page 43 Raj's special present
Narrative objective: To write a new story based on familiar patterned language.
Setting the homework: Remind the children of the book *Handa's Surprise* and the patterned language in the book that relates to the task on the homework sheet.
Differentiation: Tell the children to ask their helpers to help them spell and write the names of the fruit and the surprise at the end.
Back at school: Organise the children in pairs so that they can read their stories to one another and reveal the surprise.

Page 44 Lost!

Narrative objective: To write a new story based on familiar patterned language.

Setting the homework: Remind the children of the book *Handa's Hen* and the patterned language in the book that relates to the task on the homework sheet.

Differentiation: Tell the children to ask their helpers to help them spell and write the names of the garden objects and animals.

Back at school: Organise the children into groups of four, choosing one of the children to read the story from their homework sheet to the other children.

Link to *100 Literacy Framework Lessons Y1:* NU2, Sequence 1, Phase 2: work on the story of *Handa's Hen*.

Page 45 The Gingerbread Man

Objective: To write a new story based on familiar patterned language.

Setting the homework: Tell the children that they are going to write a new story based on the repetitive lines from 'The Gingerbread Man'. Discuss how the story might change if the characters that the Gingerbread Man met said something other than *"Stop! I want to eat you."*

Differentiation: All the children should be able to complete the homework sheet. Some will be able to tell part of a story, or a short story, while other children should try to create a new story using all the new lines.

Back at school: Organise a role play area where the children can re-enact their stories.

Link to *100 Literacy Framework Lessons Y1:* NU2, Sequence 1, Phase 1: work on the story of 'The Gingerbread Man'.

Page 46 Full stop ahead! – Core skills

Objective: To interpret a text by reading aloud with some variety of pace and emphasis.

Setting the homework: Explain to the children that they should read the story and pause when there is a full stop. Then, they should put a ring round each full stop.

Differentiation: Some children will need support from their helper to read the text.

Back at school: Using an enlarged extract, read it with the children, pausing as appropriate. Select a child to put a ring round the full stops.

Page 47 Tog the Dog – Core skills

Objective: To explore the effects of patterns of language.

Setting the homework: Explain to the children that they will read a short story about Tog the dog with their helper and that they should look for the rhyming words.

Differentiation: Some children will need support from their helper to read the story.

Back at school: Re-read the extract with the class, pausing for them to fill in the rhyming words.

Page 48 Rhyming pairs – Core skills

Objective: To spell new words using phonics as the prime approach.

Setting the homework: Explain that the children will need help in cutting out and making the cards. Show the children a set of words you have already made and choose four children to demonstrate how to play the game. Tell them that their helper should play the game with them, but that once they have mastered the game, they should play it with other members of their family and friends.

Differentiation: All children should find the game fun to play. Some whose phonological awareness is not sufficiently developed will need time in relating pronunciation to spelling. Other children could be directed to increasing the number of cards by adding other pairs of words with similar endings.

Back at school: Select children to read, say and spell some of the words from the game.

Page 49 'Ea' snap – Core skills

Objective: To recognise and use alternative ways of pronouncing graphemes.

Setting the homework: Explain to the children that they will be making and playing a game of 'Snap', looking and listening for words that have the same sound. Ensure they know the rules of the game.

Back at school: Organise for groups of children to play the game, for reinforcement.

Narrative – Unit 3 Traditional and fairy tales

Page 50 Beginnings and endings

Narrative objective: To identify beginnings and endings of stories.
Setting the homework: Explain to the children the need to read each bit of text carefully with their helper and to decide whether it would be best used for the beginning or the end of a story.
Differentiation: Some children will need greater support in reading the beginnings and endings.
Back at school: Organise children into writing groups. Ask each group to choose a beginning and an ending and use them to write a group story.

Page 51 Beginning, middle and ending

Narrative objective: To summarise the plot using beginning, middle and ending.
Setting the homework: Not all the children may have access to the internet to watch the story on the Northumberland website with their helper, so tell all the children to ask their helper if they can tell them the story of 'The Three Billy Goats Gruff'. Explain to the children that they have to read and then match the speech bubbles to the appropriate pictures and arrange them into the beginning, middle and ending of the story.
Back at school: Organise for pairs of children to watch and use the interactive version of 'The Three Billy Goats Gruff' on: http://ngfl.northumberland.gov.uk/english/goats/billygoatsgruff.html so that they can retell the story.
Link to *100 Literacy Framework Lessons Y1:* NU3, Phase 1: sequencing the story of 'The Three Billy Goats Gruff'.

Page 52 The Three Billy Goats Gruff

Narrative objective: To retell a story, organising events in sequence.
Setting the homework: Explain to the children that their helper should read the story to them so that they can retell it back or to someone else.
Differentiation: Some children will need greater assistance in the form of prompting when retelling the story, whereas other children should be able to make links between different events in the story and answer questions such as: *What happened when Big Billy Goat Gruff crossed the bridge?*
Back at school: Ask the children a number of questions which draw out their ability to make links between the events in the story.
Link to *100 Literacy Framework Lessons Y1:* NU3, Phase 1: sequencing the story of 'The Three Billy Goats Gruff'.

Page 53 The Polar Bear and the Hobyahs

Narrative objective: To retell a story, organising events in sequence.
Setting the homework: Emphasise that the point of this homework is not to be able to read the story but to be able to listen to the story being read and then to retell it. All children should ask their helpers to read the story to them.
Back at school: Choose one or two children to retell the story. One child could write the main points of the story on a flipchart.

Page 54 Finger puppets

Narrative objective: To re-enact a story using puppets.
Setting the homework: It may be helpful to ensure that the children have access at home to crayons, scissors and glue before explaining how to make the finger puppets. Not all the children may have access to the internet to watch the story on the Cbeebies website with their helper, so tell all the children to ask their helper if they can tell them the story of 'Jack and the Beanstalk'.
Back at school: Organise the children in pairs and ask them to identify and talk about the story language they used to retell their story. Select children to share some of their phrases from the story with the whole class.
Link to *100 Literacy Framework Lessons Y1:* NU3, Phase 2: re-enacting stories using puppets.

Page 55 Jack and the Beanstalk

Narrative objective: To read a playscript and adapt voices for different characters.

Setting the homework: Not all the children may have access to the internet to watch the story on the website provided, so tell the children to ask their helper if they can tell them the story of 'Jack and the Beanstalk'. Explain to the children that they have to read each part as if they were the character.

Differentiation: Most children will need support in reading the playscript, so inform the helpers to model reading the playscript with appropriate expression and help the children to read any difficult words.

Back at school: Provide a 'Jack and the Beanstalk' role-play area. Organise groups of children to re-enact the story by pretending to be characters in the story in the role-play area.

Link to *100 Literacy Framework Lessons Y1:* NU3, Phases 4 and 6: work on the story of 'Jack and the Beanstalk'.

Page 56 What happens next?

Narrative objective: To retell a traditional tale.

Setting the homework: Remind the children of the two traditional tales 'The Three Little Pigs' and 'The Three Billy Goats Gruff' and the points in the stories that the two pictures depict. Explain to the children that they have to retell the whole story to their helper, and that some children will need their helper to support them to write what happens next.

Differentiation: All children should know the traditional stories in the pictures and be able to retell the story to others. The more difficult aspect of this homework task is to write what happens next and some children will need extra support from their helper at this point.

Back at school: Organise the children into groups for retellings. In a class session, choose some children to read out their story endings.

Page 57 What's happening?

Narrative objective: To retell a story using pictures as prompts and write a story in own words.

Setting the homework: Tell the children that they should attempt to do all that is required but tell the most confident to write as much as they want to about what is happening in the picture. They may use a separate piece of paper for this.

Differentiation: Some children should concentrate on retelling the story whereas others should be encouraged to write as much as they can about the incident depicted in the picture.

Back at school: Organise for some children to retell a story to a younger child, possibly in another class. Discuss children's writing with the aim of making improvements.

Link to *100 Literacy Framework Lessons Y1:* NU3, Phase 1: retelling traditional tales.

Page 58 The Little Red Hen: a picture story

Narrative objective: To retell a story using pictures as prompts.

Setting the homework: Explain to the children that they need to look carefully at the pictures and tell the story to their helper.

Back at school: Select different children to retell the story to the class.

Link to *100 Literacy Framework Lessons Y1:* NU3, Phase 1: retelling traditional tales.

Page 59 The Little Red Hen

Narrative objective: To write a story using pictures as prompts.

Setting the homework: Explain to the children that they need to write sentences to match the pictures. Point out that there are words provided to help them.

Differentiation: All children should be encouraged to attempt writing. For those lacking in confidence or ability, ask their helper to scribe parts for them.

Back at school: Encourage children to read their sentences to the class and display the results in the classroom.

Link to *100 Literacy Framework Lessons Y1:* NU3, Phase 6: writing traditional tales in own words.

Page 60 What's wrong? – Core skills

Objective: To use syntax and context when reading for meaning.

Setting the homework: Explain to the children that they are going to be teacher and mark the mistakes. You might read the first sentence to emphasise that it does not make sense.

Back at school: Re-read the incorrect story and ask children to suggest corrections. You could enlarge the text to do so.

Page 61 The Clever Cockerel and the Crafty Fox – Core skills
Objective: To use capital letters and full stops when punctuating simple sentences.
Setting the homework: Tell the children that the sentences on the sheet make up a story but that the capital letters and full stops are missing. It is their job to punctuate the sentences correctly.
Differentiation: Some children will require a smaller selection of the less complex sentences.
Back at school: Organise the children to work in pairs checking each other's work for correct punctuation. Then, read the whole story aloud together.

Page 62 Ooh, look at that! – Core skills
Objective: To recognise and use alternative ways or pronouncing the graphemes already taught.
Setting the homework: Talk about words that include 'oo' and discuss their pronunciation. Explain that the children are going to sort 'oo' words according to their vowel sounds.
Differentiation: More confident children could be asked to find further 'oo' words in reading books to add to their lists.
Back at school: Encourage children to apply their phonic skills to reading new words.

Page 63 Phoneme sounds (1) – Core skills
Objective: To segment words into their constituent phonemes.
Setting the homework: Explain to the children that they will need to listen carefully to the sounds (phonemes) that make up the words. Use the word *phoneme*. If appropriate, remind or tell the children that the long vowel sound is the name of the letter.
Differentiation: This activity is appropriate for those children who are able to identify phonemes. Children who are not able to do so will require additional support.
Back at school: Provide a set of different words on the flipchart and choose children to segment them.

Page 64 Long vowel sounds (1) – Core skills
Objective: To recognise and use alternative ways of spelling the phonemes already taught.
Setting the homework: You will need to give the children coloured counters. Talk about the words that include different spellings of the /ie/ sound. Explain that the children are going to sort words by using different coloured counters to cover the different spellings of the sound /ie/.
Differentiation: This activity is suitable for all the children who can identify phonemes. Some children will need more adult support in identifying the spellings. An extension activity for other children would be to collect words containing the sound /ie/ from their reading books.
Back at school: Provide other word grids so that the children can play the game and develop their skills. Look for evidence of children learning these words by conducting a spelling test.

Narrative – Unit 4 Stories about fantasy worlds

Page 65 Slime World

Narrative objective: To identify objects found in settings that make them different from the world around us.

Setting the homework: Tell the children to explain to their helpers that the homework activity is about talking together in order to explore the detail in the picture, and how it differs from their own world.

Back at school: Organise the children to work in groups of four to discuss and agree on a fantasy setting they create through a collaborative painting.

Link to *100 Literacy Framework Lessons Y1:* NU4, Phase 1: work on objects that identify a setting.

Page 66 Book covers

Narrative objective: To explore fantasy settings, make predictions and express preferences.

Setting the homework: Explain to the children that it is important they should be able to talk about books, to be able to predict what a book might be about and to explain why they may prefer one book rather than another. Tell them they should talk to their helpers about what they think the books shown on the homework sheet might be about and whether or not they would like to read them.

Differentiation: Some children will need greater support from their helper when producing explanations and reasons for their preferences.

Back at school: In a whole-class shared reading lesson, show the children two different book covers. Elicit a discussion that will allow the children to practise their skills in speaking about story predictions and preferences.

Link to *100 Literacy Framework Lessons Y1:* NU4, Phase 1: predicting events in a narrative.

Page 67 What sort of story?

Narrative objective: To explore fantasy settings, make predictions and express preferences.

Setting the homework: Ask the children what 'blurbs' on books do and explain that their homework involves reading 'blurbs'. Tell the children that they will be expected to report back to the class on the discussions they have with their helpers about what sort of stories they think the books will be about.

Differentiation: Children who are less confident with books will require increased support from their helper in the form of more questioning and prompting.

Back at school: Organise children into groups so that they can share their opinions about what the books might be about. Follow this up by trying the activity in a whole-class shared reading session with some books from your classroom library.

Link to *100 Literacy Framework Lessons Y1:* NU4, Phase 1: predicting events in a narrative.

Page 68 Tell your fantasy story

Narrative objective: To orally compose an adventure narrative.

Setting the homework: Tell the children that the pictures on the homework sheet are to give them ideas and help them make predictions about what might happen. They should choose the pictures that they find most interesting and use them to create an adventure story that they can tell orally.

Differentiation: All children will need to engage in discussion with their helper, who should support them by helping them to talk about what might happen.

Back at school: Provide a role-play area where the children can re-enact their own stories.

Link to *100 Literacy Framework Lessons Y1:* NU4, Phase 2: telling an adventure narrative.

Page 69 Robot 144

Narrative objective: To retell a story orally with main events in sequence.
Setting the homework: Tell the children that this activity is to help them tell adventure stories for role play. Say that some of the words in the story are difficult but that it is a story for their helper to read to them rather than for them to read themselves.
Differentiation: Children who are interested in computers and stories about space may find the story easier to access than children less familiar with such settings.
Back at school: Provide robot suits (these could be boxes painted silver and gold to fit on arms and legs), and an appropriate role-play area where the children can re-enact the story.

Page 70 Roto and the Hullaloobs

Narrative objective: To predict how characters might look and behave.
Setting the homework: Tell the children to ask their helpers to read the extract to them so that they can listen carefully to what is happening. Also tell them that their helper will be like you and ask lots of questions about the characters.
Differentiation: The questions are differentiated in order to elicit responses that demand imagination and reasoning abilities.
Back at school: Explore the text further by asking children to predict the reactions of the characters and what might happen next in the story.

Page 71 Storyline

Narrative objective: To develop the pattern of problem and resolution in a story.
Setting the homework: Revise with the children the problem and resolution structure that often underpins a story, especially adventure stories. Tell them that the task is to predict what is happening in the pictures in order to sort out the sequence, identifying the problem and how it is solved.
Differentiation: Some children will need help in reading the words on the storyline.
Back at school: Prepare four large cards on which is written the storyline words *problem, afraid, resolution* and *happy ending*. Ask four children to stand in a line holding the cards in the order in the storyline. Using stories the children know, or are currently reading, ask them to identify the problem, why someone is afraid, the resolution and the happy ending.
Link to *100 Literacy Framework Lessons Y1*: NU4, Phase 2: work on problems and resolutions.

Page 72 Phoneme sounds (2) – Core skills

Objective: To segment words into their constituent phonemes.
Setting the homework: Explain to the children that they will have to listen carefully to the sounds that make up the word.
Differentiation: Children who have difficulty in identifying sounds will need more adult support.
Back at school: Do a spelling test containing some of the words from the homework activity.

Page 73 Long vowel sounds (2) – Core skills

Objective: To recognise and use alternative ways of spelling the phonemes already taught.
Setting the homework: You will need to give the children coloured counters. Talk about the words that include different spellings of the /oe/ sound. Explain that the children are going to sort words by using different coloured counters to cover the different spellings of the sound /oe/.
Differentiation: This activity is suitable for all the children who can identify phonemes. Some children will need more adult support in identifying the spellings. An extension activity for other children would be to collect words containing the sound /oe/ from their reading books.
Back at school: Provide other word grids so that the children can play the game and develop their skills. Look for evidence of children learning these words by conducting a spelling test.

Page 74 Spelling game – Core skills
Objective: To spell new words using phonics as the prime approach.
Setting the homework: Tell the children to ask their helper to help them make the game and play it with them. Say to the children that it is to help them practise spelling frequently used words and that they should apply their skills in phonics where appropriate when trying to read a difficult word.
Differentiation: Some children might be asked to use a smaller number of words than on the sheet, while others might be given additional words.
Back at school: Children should have opportunities to apply phonic knowledge and skills in guided reading.

Page 75 How would you feel? – Core skills
Objective: To compose and write simple sentences independently to communicate meaning.
Setting the homework: Explain to the children that they are going to write sentences to describe how they would feel if they were in the same situation as the characters in the pictures. Model an example sentence using either one of the pictures on the page or another of your own choosing. Remind the children to start their sentences with capital letters and end them with full stops.
Differentiation: All the children should attempt to describe how they would feel, but some will require greater assistance from their helper to compose the sentences.
Back at school: Organise the children in groups or pairs so that they can share each other's responses to the pictures and check their work for the correct use of capital letters and full stops.

Non-fiction – Unit 1 Labels, lists and captions

Page 76 Label the house
Non-fiction objective: To revise the purpose of labels.
Setting the homework: Explain to the children how to label a drawing using the example on the homework sheet.
Differentiation: All children should be able to use their reading skills to determine the appropriate word and use it as a label on the picture.
Back at school: Display a large picture related to a current topic and ask a group of children to label it. Ask other groups to label equipment or specific resources in the classroom.
Link to *100 Literacy Framework Lessons Y1:* NFU1, Phase 1: writing labels.

Page 77 Can you help?
Objective: To write sentence captions.
Setting the homework: Explain to the children that they will need to look carefully at the pictures and then write a sentence or caption to fit the picture.
Differentiation: Some children may need their helper to scribe the sentences for them.
Back at school: Ask selected children to share the captions they have written.
Link to *100 Literacy Framework Lessons Y1:* NFU1, Phase 1: writing captions.

Page 78 The garden centre – Core skills
Objective: To use capital letters and full stops when punctuating simple sentences.
Setting the homework: Tell the children that they are going to match captions to pictures but before doing so they must check that the sentences are correct. Ask the children to remind one another of two very important features of a sentence.
Differentiation: Some children will need the sentences reading to them.
Back at school: Use the activity to create a display. As part of the normal setting up of displays, involve the children in writing captions using complete sentences.

Non-fiction – Unit 2 Instructions

Page 79 Instruction language
Non-fiction objective: To identify simple instructions.
Setting the homework: Explain that the task involves sorting out which are instructions and which are not. Remind the children about how instructions look and what words are used.
Differentiation: Some children will need extra help in reading the instructions.
Back at school: Select two children to explain their reasoning for the choices they made.

Page 80 How to make a jungle scene
Non-fiction objective: To read and follow simple instructions.
Setting the homework: Explain to the children that they will need to read and follow instructions to make a picture with a helper. It may be helpful to ensure at first that the children have access at home to crayons, scissors and glue to do the activity.
Back at school: Ask the children to share their completed pictures. If children are going to be undertaking the activity on page 82, ensure that the pictures are kept in a safe place as they will be needed for that activity.

Page 81 How to make a fruit salad
Non-fiction objective: To write simple instructions in the form of captions.
Setting the homework: Explain to the children that they are going to write the instructions for making a fruit salad by using the pictures on the homework sheet and using the helpful words to begin their sentences.
Differentiation: Some children will need their helper to support them when writing a sentence.
Back at school: Organise the children into groups so that they can read and compare each other's instructions.
Link to *100 Literacy Framework Lessons Y1:* NFU2, Phase 3: writing instructions.

Page 82 My jungle scene – Core skills
Objective: To compose and write simple sentences.
Setting the homework: Please note that this activity works with that on page 80 and is dependent on the children having completed that activity first. Explain to the children that they are going to write sentences to describe the jungle scene that they assembled for a previous homework. Ensure that the children have their previous work of a jungle scene to take home with them.
Differentiation: All children should be encouraged to attempt writing. Some children will need their helpers to scribe for them.
Back at school: Ask selected children to show their drawings and read out their sentences. Display the results.

Page 83 Change the word – Core skills
Objective: To spell words using phonics as the prime approach.
Setting the homework: Ensure that children realise that they need to place a different vowel letter in between the consonants to make different words. Tell them that the letters 'b' and 'h' should be tried instead of the 'p'. They are not to be used in the middle.
Differentiation: This activity is suitable for children who can identify all vowel letters and make the short vowel sound. They will also need to know some consonant phonemes. Other children will need plenty of support.
Back at school: Play the game in class and ask different children to read the words made.

Page 84 Blend a word – Core skills
Objective: To apply phonic knowledge and skills as the prime approach to reading and spelling.
Setting the homework: Remind the children of the phonics work they are doing in school.
Differentiation: For some children this might be new while others may be confident at blending letters together and therefore this is reinforcement. Some children could be given further similar words to read.
Back at school: Children should apply their phonic knowledge and skills to decoding new words.

Non-fiction – Unit 3 Recounts, dictionary

Page 85 School day (1)
Objective: To learn appropriate vocabulary for ordering a recount.
Setting the homework: Discuss with the children how questions can help in the telling of events that have happened such as going on a school trip or getting ready for bedtime – and provide some examples. Tell the children that their helper is going to ask some questions that will help them order what happens in a school day.
Differentiation: Most children will be able to recognise the sequence of events of the school day and be able to use vocabulary associated with recounts appropriately.
Back at school: Organise the children to work in pairs where each are given a task of recounting a daily routine such as brushing teeth, getting ready for school, bedtime, to tell their partner.
Link to *100 Literacy Framework Lessons Y1:* NFU3, Phase 3, Day 4 : sequencing a recount.

Page 86 School day (2)
Non-fiction objective: To order events in a recount.
Setting the homework: Remind the children about the order in which to tell a recount in relation to matching the captions to the pictures on the homework sheet. Ask the helpers to alert the children to the first words of the sentences which serve to organise the sequence of events.
Differentiation: Most children will be able to recognise the sequence of events in the school day.
Back at school: Enable children to record their day at school in photographs with accompanying writing that draws on recount vocabulary.
Link to *100 Literacy Framework Lessons Y1:* NFU3, Phase 3, Day 4: sequencing a recount.

Page 87 My day at school
Non-fiction objective: To make own simple recounts in sentences using past tense and time connectives.
Setting the homework: Explain the homework sheet, telling the children to discuss their school day with their helper.
Differentiation: The writing frame and familiar setting should allow most children to complete this task. Some children may need their helper to write for them.
Back at school: Organise the children in pairs so that they can compare their writing about their day at school.
Link to *100 Literacy Framework Lessons Y1:* NFU3, Phase 3, Day 5: writing a recount.

Page 88 Indexes
Objective: To understand alphabetical order in texts.
Setting the homework: Explain to the children that they will be sorting words into alphabetical order for an index like the ones they have seen in information books.
Differentiation: All children will need support in reading new and unfamiliar words.
Back at school: Provide a group activity task where the children use indexes and thereby further their understanding.
Link to *100 Literacy Framework Lessons Y1:* NFU3, Phase 3, Day 1: alphabetical order.

Page 89 Using dictionaries
Non-fiction objective: To use dictionaries and understand their alphabetical organisation.
Setting the homework: Equip children with simple dictionaries if they do not have a dictionary at home. Explain to the children that they are to find the meanings of the words on the homework sheet using the dictionary as they do in group activities and shared reading.
Differentiation: Some children who find writing difficult will need greater assistance when writing sentences.
Back at school: Extend dictionary work by giving pairs of children a dictionary from which to locate words which you call out. Select pairs to read out the meanings of the words found.
Link to *100 Literacy Framework Lessons Y1:* NFU3, Phase 3, Day 1: alphabetical order.

Page 90 Extend a word – Core skills

Objective: To apply phonic knowledge and skills as the prime approach to reading and spelling.
Setting the homework: Remind the children of the phonics work they are doing in school.
Differentiation: For some children this might be new while others may be confident at blending letters together and therefore this is reinforcement. Some children could be given further similar words to read.
Back at school: Children should apply their phonic knowledge and skills to decoding new words.

Non-fiction – Unit 4 Information texts

Page 91 Question or not?

Non-fiction objective: To identify questions.
Setting the homework: Discuss with the children the different inflection and expression we use when asking a question and use examples to make the point: *We are going to the zoo* (statement); *Are we going to the zoo?* (question). Explain to the children that they should read the sentences aloud in order to hear the questions.
Back at school: Provide further statements and questions on the flipchart ready for children to provide the correct punctuation.

Page 92 Ask a question

Non-fiction objective: To write own questions.
Setting the homework: Explain to the children that the point of the homework is to be able to ask questions rather than answer questions. Talk about why this is an important skill in that reading involves the reader asking questions as well as finding answers.
Back at school: Collect all the different questions the children have raised and display them on a large sheet in large print so that children can read them. Use the questions at a further shared reading or writing lesson.

Page 93 Questions, questions

Non-fiction objective: To write own questions.
Setting the homework: Tell the children they are going to ask questions that can be answered by looking at the picture. Give an example: *How many children are riding scooters? Which shop is next to the butcher's shop?*
Differentiation: Some children will require their helper to write for them, but all children should be encouraged to attempt to write for themselves.
Back at school: Display an enlarged version of the picture of the street and share some of the questions that have already been made. Elicit further questions from the children which could be placed around the picture.

Page 94 All about seeds

Non-fiction objective: To use an information text to find answers.
Setting the homework: Explain to the children that their helper should read 'All about seeds' to them and then they should read it again with the helper before answering the questions. Encourage them, when answering the questions, to look for key words in the text rather than re-reading the whole text.
Differentiation: All the children should be able to discern the relevant information from having the text 'All about seeds' read to them. Some may need help in completing their written answers.
Back at school: Use a simple test for further comprehension work in small groups.
Link to *100 Literacy Framework Lessons Y1*: NFU4, Phase 1: using an information book to find answers.

Page 95 Favourite animals

Non-fiction objective: To use an information text to find answers.
Setting the homework: Read through the homework sheet explaining to the children how to read the chart.
Differentiation: The chart is 'child friendly' and all children should attempt the homework. Some will require support when reading the questions.
Back at school: Display an empty version of the chart in order to determine the favourite animals of children in the class.

Page 96 My dad
Non-fiction objective: To use an information text to find answers.
Setting the homework: Explain what the chart is about, and what the children have to do.
Differentiation: All children should be able to use the chart to locate information, but some will need extra help in reading the sentences.
Back at school: Organise children in groups so that they can check each other's work.

Page 97 Fiction or non-fiction?
Non-fiction objective: To sort books into fiction and non-fiction.
Setting the homework: Ensure that the children know the terms 'fiction' and 'non-fiction' and have some concept of their differences. Discuss what the sheet requires them to do, and encourage them to explain to their helper why they made their decisions.
Differentiation: All children should be encouraged to explain their decisions.
Back at school: Create a display of fiction and non-fiction books and ask children to label them.
Link to *100 Literacy Framework Lessons Y1:* NFU4, Phase 2: comparing fiction and non-fiction.

Page 98 What I know about my mum
Non-fiction objective: To record information as a spidergram.
Setting the homework: The homework sheet is quite easy to follow, so a brief explanation is all that should be required. Be sensitive to children's varying home situations. If appropriate, adapt the sheet so the child is writing about someone else they know well.
Back at school: Discuss with the children the features of the language: for example, short rather than long descriptions.
Link to *100 Literacy Framework Lessons Y1:* NFU3, Phase 3: using a report skeleton to write notes.

Page 99 What is Dad thinking?
Non-fiction objective: To write a report supported by pictures.
Setting the homework: Tell the children that they should all attempt to write sentences that describe what Dad wants to do instead of working in the house.
Back at school: Ask children to take turns to read out their sentences.

Page 100 Crocodiles
Non-fiction objective: To discuss suitable subheadings for a report.
Setting the homework: This activity should be used when children have experience of reading subheadings in an information book. Explain to the children that they are going to read an information text called 'Crocodiles' then decide what might make good subheadings for each part of the text.
Back at school: Discuss children's ideas and vote on the best subheadings.

Page 101 Sentences to punctuate – Core skills
Objective: To use capital letters and full stops when punctuating simple sentences.
Setting the homework: Tell the children what the sentences are about and tell them about the punctuation features you want them to use.
Differentiation: You may wish to omit the questions for less confident children.
Back at school: Choose some of the children to read out the sentences with expression. Ensure that they use correct inflection for questions.

Page 102 Capital letters – Core skills
Objective: To use capital letters when punctuating simple sentences.
Setting the homework: Tell the children that capital letters are missing from the four sentences on the sheet. They should read the sentences, then write them in the space provided with the capital letters in the right place.
Differentiation: All children should be able to do the task, although some will need extra support when reading the sentences.
Back at school: Provide a selection of names of teachers, staff and helpers in school without capital letters so that children can supply them. Recap on different uses of capital letters.

Page 103 Charlotte, Charles and Chloe – Core skills

Objective: To recognise and use alternative ways of pronouncing the graphemes already taught.
Setting the homework: Explain to the children that they will be identifying words which include the digraph 'ch' and then sorting them into different categories according to the way in which 'ch' is sounded in each word. You may wish to practise identifying and categorising such words in school before setting the homework – for example, check that the children understand that *Christmas* sounds like *Chloe* because of the hard 'c' sound at the beginning of the word.
Differentiation: Some children could be asked to do the homework using other, more challenging texts.
Back at school: As a quick assessment of whether all the children have been able to complete this activity, provide an enlarged version of the sentences and ask them to identify and categorise the 'ch' words.

Page 104 Chef's chocolate – Core skills

Objective: To recognise and use alternative ways of pronouncing the graphemes already taught.
Setting the homework: Explain to the children that they will be asked to look at a collection of words and then sort them according to the sound which 'ch' makes in each. They should be encouraged to find further 'ch' words and sort these too.
Differentiation: Some children might be given a more limited selection of words or could have some of the words categorised for them on an amended version of the homework sheet.
Back at school: Play a matching game with the whole class. Give each child a card with a 'ch' word printed on it and ask the children to take turns to stand up and show and say their words. All of the children who have a word with a similar 'ch' sound should hold up their cards so that you may check if they have understood the different pronunciations.

Non-fiction – Unit 5 Recount (fact and fiction)

Page 105 Sequence

Non-fiction objective: To sequence events using time connectives.
Setting the homework: Remind the children of the key words at the beginning of each sentence which will help them detect the right order.
Back at school: Organise for someone to brush their teeth while another child reads the recount. Ask the children: *Has anything been left out in the written account?*
Link to *100 Literacy Framework Lessons Y1:* NFU5, Phase 1: sequencing events based on own experience.

Page 106 Growing plants from seeds

Non-fiction objective: To orally compose a recount, sequencing events.
Setting the homework: Tell the children that the pictures on the sheet are jumbled and need putting in the correct order. Remind them to explain their choices to their helper.
Back at school: Provide further sets of for pictures, for example: brushing teeth (putting toothpaste on brush; brushing teeth; rinsing mouth; smiling, showing clean teeth); making a sandwich (buttering bread, putting filling on, cutting in half, eating sandwich). In pairs, children place them in the correct order and explain their choices.

Page 107 Getting dressed
Non-fiction objective: To write a recount using time connectives.
Setting the homework: Explain to the children that they should use the time connectives they have been using in lessons to write about getting dressed. Tell the children they are first going to choose the clothes to put on the child in the picture remembering what went on first, then, next and so on.
Differentiation: Some children may only orally describe the order in which the child was dressed. Other children should be able to write the sequence using the time connectives to help them start their sentences.
Back at school: In shared writing, model writing the recount of getting dressed involving the children in choosing the appropriate time connectives.
Link to *100 Literacy Framework Lessons Y1:* NFU5, Phase 2: writing a recount using time connectives.

Page 108 What happens when?
Non-fiction objective: To write a recount using time connectives.
Setting the homework: Explain that the children's helpers will need to view 'Growing plants' with them from the website on the sheet. Those who don't have a computer at home could do it with their helper in school using the school computer.
Differentiation: Most children should attempt to complete the sentences to show what happens to the plant as it is watered. Some children may want to explore what happens when the blind is drawn.
Back at school: Organise for the children to work in pairs so that they read their sequence of sentences to one another.
Link to *100 Literacy Framework Lessons Y1:* NFU5, Phase 2: writing a recount using time connectives.

Page 109 Matching sounds – Core skills
Objective: To apply phonic knowledge and skills as the prime approach to reading and spelling words.
Setting the homework: Show the children examples of words and sentences like those on the homework sheet and do a few together so that they understand how to set about their task.
Back at school: As a quick assessment of whether all the children have been able to complete this activity, do some more examples on the board and ask children to match the sounds.

Page 110 Odd one out – Core skills
Objective: To recognise and use alternative ways of spelling the phonemes already taught.
Setting the homework: Show the children examples of sets of words with highlighted graphemes in which one word has a different sound from the others.
Differentiation: Some children could make up further sets of words similar to those on the homework sheet.
Back at school: Ask the children to identify odd words out from sets of words you have produced on the board. Check that all children are able to hear the vowel phonemes and distinguish between them.

Poetry – Unit 1 Using the senses

Page 111 How does it feel?
Poetry objective: To find simple words and phrases to describe what they can feel.
Setting the homework: Ensure that the helpers know to provide or make a 'feely bag' in preparation for this activity and to select three or four items to use in the feely bag.
Differentiation: Some children might want to extend their collection of words and phrases into a poem.
Back at school: Organise the children to work in pairs in order to play a guessing game. Can their partner guess what the object is from the descriptions they have written?
Link to *100 Literacy Framework Lessons Y1:* PU1, Phase 1, Day 1: describing how materials feel.

Page 112 Create a poem
Poetry objective: To fit descriptive words into a simple poetry frame.
Setting the homework: Read through the instructions and models on the homework sheet with all the children. Ask two children to read the two exemplar poems aloud to the class.
Differentiation: Some children should be able to do this activity by themselves, whereas others will need to discuss the focus of their poem, at length, with their helper.
Back at school: Make time, possibly over a few days, for children to read aloud their poems to the rest of the class. A class anthology could be made.

Page 113 Be a poet
Poetry objective: To fit descriptive words into a simple poetry frame.
Setting the homework: Explain to the children that they are going to be poets and write a poem about their favourite food. Explain that by finding words to describe its colour, sound, feel, smell and taste they will be able to use them to construct a poem based on the 'diamond' model you should show them.
Differentiation: Some children may find the model restrictive and should be encouraged to be creative in constructing more elaborate poems.
Back at school: Organise a poetry reading time each day for a week so that the children can read aloud their poems to the whole class.
Link to *100 Literacy Framework Lessons Y1:* PU1, Phase 1: food and the senses as a stimulus for writing poetry.

Page 114 Sort the rhymes – Core skills
Objective: To recognise and use alternative ways of spelling the phonemes already taught.
Setting the homework: Explain to the children that they have to sort the rhyming words by their spellings.
Differentiation: Some children should be directed to the additional activity of finding other spelling patterns for the rhyme.
Back at school: Make an enlarged grid for the classroom with columns marked 'ear', 'air', 'ere', 'eir', are to which children can add words as they find them during reading activities.

P115 Sounds of the city – Core skills
Objective: To recognise and use alternative ways of spelling the phonemes already taught.
Setting the homework: Explain to the children that they will be reading a poem to see which words rhyme and to explore the different spellings of /s/.
Differentiation: Some children's phonological awareness may not be sufficiently developed to enable them to investigate a range of graphemes for the same phoneme. It may be preferable to focus on a limited number of graphemes such as only 's' and 'ss'.
Back at school: Read the poem with the class and, using an enlarged copy, ask different children to highlight the letters making /s/.

Poetry – Unit 2 Pattern and rhyme

Page 116 Time for...?

Poetry objective: To read and respond to rhyme.
Setting the homework: Explain to the children that they will read a poem with their helper and look for rhyming words.
Back at school: Re-read the poem with the class and pause for them to add the rhyming words.

Page 117 Little Samantha's day

Poetry objective: To read and respond to rhyme.
Setting the homework: Explain to the children that they have to re-order some sentences that rhyme in order to make a rhyming story.
Differentiation: Some children will need the sentences reading to them and greater assistance from their helper when putting them in sequence.
Back at school: Select children to read the rhyming story.

Page 118 Ill in bed

Poetry objective: To read and respond to rhyme.
Setting the homework: Discuss with the children what the poem is about and explain how they have to put sentences in the correct order and to use the rhyme endings to help them.
Back at school: With the children read the poem, omitting the rhyme ending in order that the children can offer the rhyming words. Ask one child to read the poem while others provide a 'still' of one of the scenes.

Page 119 One to ten – Core skills

Objective: To recognise and use alternative ways of spelling the phonemes already taught.
Setting the homework: Explain to the children that the poems are simple ones that help people to remember the order of the numbers one to ten. Ask them to look at the rhyming words at the end of each pair of lines.
Differentiation: There are further lines for 'One, two, buckle my shoe', going up to 20. Some children could be given these to read and be asked to learn the spellings of numbers 11 to 20. Rhymes for these numbers may be limited given that so many end with 'teen'.
Back at school: Conduct a shared writing session in which the whole class helps you to write an alternative version of one of the rhymes. Note the children's awareness of rhymes and of the different ways in which these may sometimes be spelled.

Page 120 Time to rhyme – Core skills

Objective: To read and spell words that include common digraphs.
Setting the homework: Talk with the children about rhyme and then relate this directly to words which include 'wh' and/or 'ph'. Ask them to match other words with similar rhymes to the 'wh' and 'ph' words.
Differentiation: Some children may need to be given fewer and simpler words to work on. These might be limited to high frequency 'wh-' words.
Back at school: Make an enlarged version of the chart from the homework sheet and incorporate the words from the sheet that rhyme and others suggested by the children. The chart could be added to over a period of weeks, as new words arise in lessons.

Page 121 Pick a pair – Core skills

Objective: To read and spell words that include adjacent consonants.
Setting the homework: Explain that the children will need help in cutting out the words and making them into cards. Remind the children of the importance of phoneme sounds in words in order to help them become better spellers and ask them to blend the sounds together if they encounter difficulty in reading the words.
Differentiation: All the children will be able to play the game, but some will need greater assistance when blending phonemes together.
Back at school: Carry out a spelling test to see if children know the words.

Poetry – Unit 3 Poems on a theme

Page 122 Have you seen the crocodile?
Poetry objective: To respond to a simple, patterned poem.
Setting the homework: Explain to the children that they will need to look carefully at the pictures to see which animal words they need to write.
Differentiation: Some children may need helpers to scribe the words.
Back at school: Examine children's writing carefully and display examples.

Page 123 The Bear's Just Had Twins!
Poetry objective: To explore a simple, patterned poem.
Setting the homework: Tell the children that they can ask their helper to assist in the reading of the poem, but that they should try to predict the rhyme ending themselves.
Back at school: Choose some of the children to read the poem omitting the endings for others to guess.

Page 124 Create an animal poem
Poetry objective: To write a simple text within an appropriate frame.
Setting the homework: Read through the instructions and model on the homework sheet with the children, pointing out the illustration and words used to describe the caterpillar.
Back at school: Make a class anthology, for example: *Class 1's Book of Animal Poems*.

Page 125 Capital letters hunt – Core skills
Objective: To identify capital letters in names.
Setting the homework: Explain to the children that they are going on a hunt – to find capital letters for names. They are going to read a bit of *Slinky Malinki*, then put a ring around every capital letter that begins someone's name.
Back at school: Display the extract (enlarged) and ask different children to underline all the names and then put a ring round the first letter of each name.

Page 126 Slinky Malinki – Core skills
Objective: To apply phonic knowledge and skills as the prime approach to reading unfamiliar words.
Setting the homework: Explain to the children that they will read an extract from *Slinky Malinki* with a helper and then they will need to re-read looking for the listed words.
Differentiation: Some children will need support from a helper to read the story.
Back at school: Display an enlarged copy of the extract. Randomly give out word cards to the children and, as you read the extract, ask each one in turn to hold up their card when they hear the corresponding word.

Page 127 Pussy Cat, Pussy Cat – Core skills
Objective: To recognise and use alternative ways of spelling the phonemes already taught.
Setting the homework: Tell the children to enjoy the poem. Explain that they are going to listen for the /ee/ sound as in *me, tea,* and *tree* and the /ai/ sound as in *train* and *say* in order to make a collection of words containing those sounds which can then be sorted by the spelling patterns into the grids.
Differentiation: Some children will need greater assistance to identify the sounds. Others could collect words containing those sounds from their reading book.
Back at school: Display extended versions of the grids to include further spellings of the sounds, for example, 'ey' as in *key* and 'a–e' as in *make* and 'ay' as in *play* in order to extend the children's awareness of the different spelling patterns.

NARRATIVE

Name   Date

Identify the characters

◼ Read the extracts in the boxes. Can you identify the characters from *Amazing Grace*?

She hid inside the wooden horse at the gates of Troy…

she crossed the Alps with Hannibal and a hundred elephants…

she sailed the seven seas

    with a peg-leg

       and a parrot.

This extract is about _____

"Lots of you want to be Peter Pan, so we'll have to have auditions. We'll choose the parts next Monday."

The person speaking in this extract is _____

"It seems that Natalie is another one who don't know nothing," she said. "You can be anything you want, Grace, if you put your mind to it."

The person speaking in this extract is _____

Text extracts © 1991, Mary Hoffman.

Dear helper
Objective: To identify characters from the text.
Task: Your child will have read *Amazing Grace* at school. With your child read each of the extracts above and ask your child to identify the character and talk about what is happening.

PHOTOCOPIABLE ◼SCHOLASTIC

www.scholastic.co.uk

Name	Date

Identify the settings

◼ Read the extracts from *Amazing Grace*. Can you identify the settings? Talk about the questions with your helper.

> When there was no-one else around, Grace played all the parts herself. She was a cast of thousands. Paw-Paw the cat usually helped out.
>
> And sometimes she could persuade Ma and Nana to join in, when they weren't too busy. Then she was Doctor Grace and their lives were in her hands.

1. Where is this part of the story set?
2. How does this setting help Grace to play?

> Outside it said, "ROSALIE WILKINS IN ROMEO AND JULIET" in beautiful sparkling lights.
>
> "Are we going to the ballet, Nana?" asked Grace.
>
> "We are, Honey, but I want you to look at these pictures first."

3. Where is this part of the story set?
4. Why will this help Grace to become Peter Pan?

> Then they had to choose Peter Pan.
>
> Grace knew exactly what to do – and all the words to say. It was a part she had often played at home. All the children voted for her.
>
> "You were great," said Natalie.

5. Where is this part of the story set?
6. Why did the children vote for Grace?

Text extracts © 1991, Mary Hoffman.

Dear helper

Objective: To identify the main settings where the story *Amazing Grace* takes place.

Task: The extracts above show the three main settings for the story, home, theatre and school. Read the texts with your child to identify the main settings for the story. The additional questions enable you to explore the significance of the settings to the story.

NARRATIVE

Name   Date

Describing characters

■ Read the descriptions of the characters and draw pictures to show what you think they look like.

■ Write some words to describe the characters in the boxes.

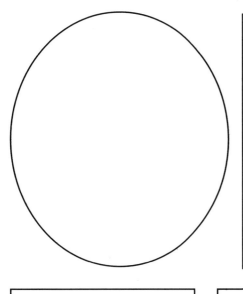

Grandma keeps an allotment. She enjoys growing vegetables and fruit and grows so many that she gives lots away to friends and neighbours.

She knows a lot about plants and animals and she is very careful not to harm wildlife. She does not spray with chemicals and does not leave harmful rubbish lying around.

Rose helps Grandma in the allotment nearly everyday.

Rose enjoys learning about plants and animals and is always eager to follow Grandma's example by taking care to keep the allotment a safe place for animals. Rose enjoys nothing better than feeling busy and helpful. She makes sure that she puts the gardening tools that she has been using back in the shed and picks up litter that might have been blown in so that the allotment looks tidy.

Dear helper
Objective: To provide words to describe the characters.
Task: Read together the descriptions of Grandma and Rose and discuss words that best describe their characters. Write the words in the boxes provided. Add more boxes for more words.

Name	Date

Story puppets

■ Make four character puppets by drawing faces in the circles. Use the puppets to help you tell a story.

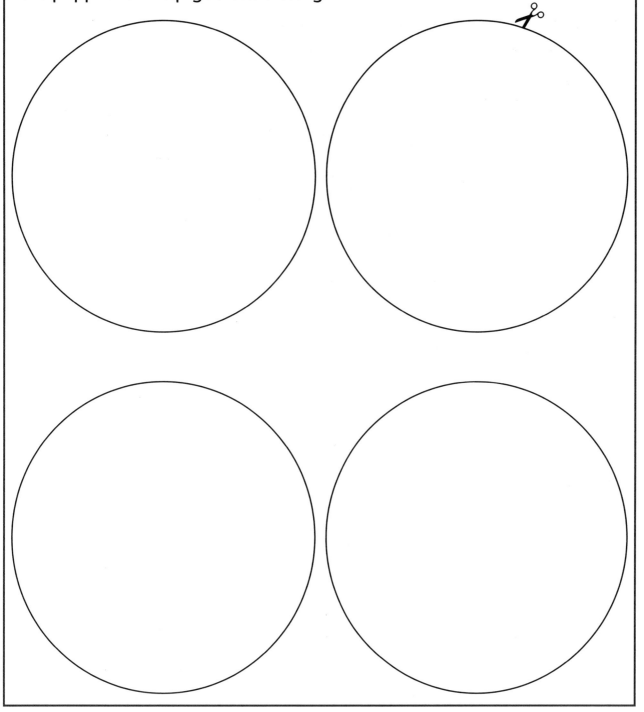

Dear helper
Objective: To describe and draw characters for telling a story.
Task: Help your child to draw the faces of four characters for telling a story. These might be family, friends, carers, neighbours. Encourage your child to provide as much detail as possible so that their drawings capture the characteristics. Stick the drawings onto lollipop sticks. The story could be from personal memory, a story that they know from school or one that they make up.

NARRATIVE

Name   Date

Tell a story, write a story

◗ The picture of children playing in the playground will be familiar to you. Think about things that have happened in your playground and tell the story to your helper.

◗ Ask your helper to help you write the story in the space underneath the picture.

◗ Write your story here:

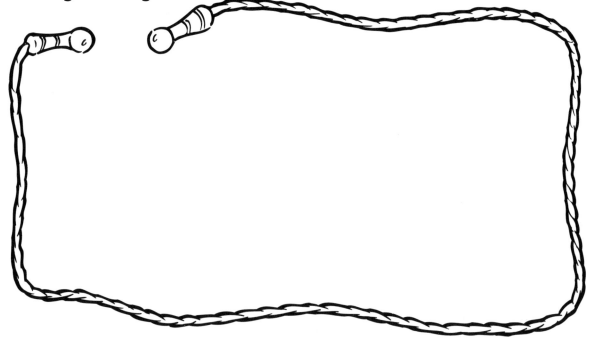

Illustrations © Theresa Tibbetts/Beehive Illustration.

Dear helper
Objective: To write a story using a familiar setting.
Task: Encourage your child to tell you about things that have happened during playtime, using the picture as a stimulus for ideas if necessary. Translating what is said into writing is difficult and your child will need you to help them to compose the story.

PHOTOCOPIABLE ■SCHOLASTIC
www.scholastic.co.uk

Name	Date

What's the story?

◼ Look at the picture and talk with your helper about what is happening.

◼ Write a short story about it on a separate sheet of paper. Which bit of the picture will you use to start your story?

Dear helper

Objective: To use a picture to write a simple story.

Task: Talk about what is happening in the picture. Discuss where the story might start and how it is going to end. Then, help your child to write a short story based on the events in the picture. If necessary, write for your child, reading the story together as you go along.

Name _____ Date _____

Draw a picture, write a sentence

■ Finish the sentences below. Draw the pictures in the boxes.

❑ Draw a picture of Grace pretending to be a character in a story.
Grace chose to play boys' parts because

_____

_____

❑ Draw a picture of what Grace saw when she went to the ballet.
At the ballet Grace saw

_____

_____

❑ Draw a picture showing Grace as Peter Pan.
Grace was chosen for the part of Peter Pan because

_____

_____

Dear helper
Objective: To write three simple sentences for the story *Amazing Grace*.
Task: Your child has read the story *Amazing Grace* in class. If possible, read the story with your child and then look carefully at the pictures that show Grace: pretending to be characters in stories; Grace with Nana going to the ballet; Grace auditioning and getting the part of Peter Pan. Help your child to draw a picture and compose and write a simple sentence that helps tell the whole story.

Name _____   Date _____

Sh, sh, sh!

- Add **sh** to the spaces.
- Then read and say the word.

_____e	_____ow	_____ake
_____ed	_____ape	_____ut
_____ell	_____ore	_____ine
swi_____	wa_____	cra_____
pu_____	fre_____	_____ould
sun_____ine	wi_____	sea_____ore

- Write some sentences using some of the words.

_____

_____

_____

_____

Illustrations © Theresa Tibbetts/Beehive Illustration.

Dear helper

Objective: To read and spell words that contain the 'sh' sound and to use them in a sentence.

Task: Help your child to complete the spellings of the words above. They should then read each one aloud to you. Choose some of the words with your child and use them to make sentences.

Jumbled words

■ Put the words in these sentences in the right order, remembering that a sentence starts with a capital letter and ends with a full stop. Write your sentences on the lines underneath.

riding bikes. are Two boys

_____

eating ice cream. an is girl A

_____

dog The is the chasing cat.

_____

old walking An is his dog. man

_____

feeding chicks. her The is bird

_____

newspapers. A man selling is

_____

Illustrations © Theresa Tibbetts/Beehive Illustration.

Dear helper
Objective: To re-order words to make sense.
Task: Support your child by discussing all the things that are happening in the picture. Then, help to sort out the words into the right order. Remind your child about starting sentences with capital letters and ending with full stops.

Spot the stops!

◼ Read the story.

◼ Look for all the full stops and put a ring round them.

Jonathan James could not get to sleep. He lay in his bed listening to the clock chime downstairs. He heard it chime eight times. Eight o'clock. He heard the music on the television which meant that his favourite programme had just finished. He had been sent to bed early for arguing and fighting with his sister, Susan. He heard her climb the stairs and go to her bedroom. It wasn't fair – she had been allowed to watch TV.

He must have fallen asleep because the next thing he knew his mother was calling him. Time to get up. It was eight o'clock. He had to eat his breakfast quickly and rush to school. His mum kept telling him to walk more quickly. He arrived just in time as the school bell rang. It was nine o'clock.

◼ Copy a sentence from the story. Remember to put a capital letter at the beginning and a full stop at the end!

Illustrations © Theresa Tibbetts/Beehive Illustration.

Dear helper

Objective: To recognise full stops when reading.

Task: First, read the story to your child. Then, read it again with your child, pausing at the full stops. Ask your child to put a ring around all the full stops. To reinforce work done at school, ask your child why the full stops are there (to show it is the end of a sentence). Now, help your child to write a sentence from the story, making sure that they remember to use a capital letter to begin and a full stop to finish the sentence.

Letter sounds

- Say each letter sound you hear in the following words.
- Use a pencil to draw a line between the sounds.

p / l / a / n / k

blink   blast   plump

drift   flint   drink

flask   grand   slept

spend   frost   twist

Illustrations © Theresa Tibbetts/Beehive Illustration.

Dear helper
Objective: To help identify letter sounds in words for spelling.
Task: Help your child to make the sound of each letter in order to blend them together to make the sound of the whole word. Drawing a pencil line between each sound will help your child to distinguish the individual letter sounds for spelling.

NARRATIVE

Name	Date

Mr. Bear

■ Read the story and make Mr. Bear sound very cross!

Text extract and illustration © 1982, Jill Murphy.

Mr. Bear was tired
Mrs. Bear was tired
and
Baby Bear was tired…

…so they all went to bed.

Mrs. Bear fell asleep.
Mr. Bear didn't.

Mrs. Bear began to snore.
"SNORE," went Mrs. Bear,
"SNORE, SNORE, SNORE."
"Oh NO!" said Mr. Bear,
"I can't stand THIS."
So he got up and went to
sleep in Baby Bear's room.

Dear helper
Objective: To read with expression.
Task: Read this extract from *Peace at Last* to your child, using as much expression as possible. Ask your child to try to read it with you. Then, ask your child to read it on their own using the correct expression.

NARRATIVE

Name

Date

Peace at Last

■ Look at the pictures. Retell the story using pictures and the words: "Oh, NO!" said Mr. Bear, "I can't stand THIS."

Story summary: Mr. Bear could not sleep. Mrs. Bear was snoring. He tried sleeping in Baby Bear's room, but Baby Bear was pretending to be an aeroplane. Then Mr. Bear went downstairs. He tried the chair in the living room, then the kitchen. That did not work so he went outside and tried the garden and even the car. Finally he went back to his bed just as it was time to get up.

Illustrations © 1982, Jill Murphy.

Dear helper
Objective: To read the repeating phrase in the story.
Task: Your child has been reading the story *Peace at Last* at school. Encourage your child to use the sequence of pictures above as prompts for retelling the story. For each picture, they should include the repeating phrase, pointing to the words as they read.

PHOTOCOPIABLE ■SCHOLASTIC
www.scholastic.co.uk

Name   Date

Name the story

■ Read the repeating lines from four well-known stories. Can you identify the stories? Who is speaking?

"Run, run as fast as you can, you can't catch me I'm the Gingerbread Man!"

"Little pigs, little pigs, let me come in."
  "No, no. Not by the hair on our chinny chin chins."
  "I'll huff and I'll puff and I'll blow your house down."

"Where are you going?"
  "The sky is falling down and I am going to tell the king."
  "Then I will come too."

Trip-trap, trip-trap, went his hooves over the bridge.
  "Who goes trip-trap, trip-trap, over my bridge?"

Illustrations © Theresa Tibbetts/Beehive Illustration.

Dear helper
Objective: To read aloud the extracts and identify the stories.
Task: Help your child to read the repeating phrase from traditional stories. Can your child guess which stories they are from? ('The Gingerbread Man', 'The Three Little Pigs', 'Chicken Licken', 'The Three Billy Goats Gruff'). It may help to retell the stories in your own words or find online versions of the stories, for example www.bbc.co.uk/cbeebies/stories/colour/gingerbreadman.shtml

■ SCHOLASTIC **PHOTOCOPIABLE**
www.scholastic.co.uk
100 LITERACY HOMEWORK ACTIVITIES · YEAR 1   **41**

NARRATIVE

| Name | Date |

Crazy animals

- Cut along the solid black lines and arrange the five pieces on top of each other. Staple the book together through the shaded area.
- When the pages are turned, new animals will appear like the one at the bottom of the page.

	kanga
	roo
	hedge
	hog
	arma
	dillo
	ele
	phant
	porcu
	pine

	hedge
	roo

Dear helper
Objective: To create new creature names by mixing and making animal names.
Task: Your child will know the story of *The Other Ark* from school. After making the 'half and half' book with your child, use it together to make up crazy animals. Talk about making more crazy animals by adding more pages. Discuss with your child what your new creatures might look like, what they might eat, where they might live and how they might behave.

PHOTOCOPIABLE **SCHOLASTIC**
www.scholastic.co.uk

Name   Date

Raj's special present

Raj is going to visit his friend in hospital and wants to take him something special. What will he take?

◼ Look at each picture and fill in the missing words to complete the sentences. The first one is done for you. Draw the last picture.

Will he like **plums** or will he like **peaches**?

Will he like _____ or will he like _____ ?

Will _____ or will _____ ?

I know! He will like some _____ !

Illustrations © Theresa Tibbetts/Beehive Illustration.

Dear helper

Objective: To write simple sentences based on patterns in familiar stories.

Task: Help your child to spell and write the words shown in the pictures. Your child will have read the story *Handa's Surprise* at school. Help your child to make connections between the patterned language of *Handa's Surprise* and the activity above.

NARRATIVE

Name	Date

Lost!

Geeta has lost her cat, Pixie and asks her friend Sim to help find it. Where can she be?

■ Provide your own ideas to complete the sentences. Make the story using the repeated sentence patterns.

They hunted round _____

"I can see two _____"

"But where's Pixie?"

They peered under _____

"I can see three _____"

"But where's Pixie?"

They peeped behind _____

"I can see four _____"

"But where's Pixie?"

They searched round _____

"I can see five _____"

"But where's Pixie?"

"What's that?"

Illustrations © Theresa Tibbetts/Beehive Illustration.

Dear helper
Objective: To invent sentences based on a pattern in a familiar story, *Handa's Hen*.
Task: Your child will have read *Handa's Hen* at school. Help your child make connections between the patterned language as used in *Handa's Hen* and the activity above.

PHOTOCOPIABLE **SCHOLASTIC**
www.scholastic.co.uk

Name	Date

The Gingerbread Man

■ Everyone in the story of 'The Gingerbread Man' said "Stop! I want to eat you!" to the Gingerbread Man except the crafty fox who said "Stop! I want to talk to you." Imagine what the story might have been if the characters had said something else.

■ Choose a good word from the box to fill in the missing word in the sentences.

The old woman said "Stop! I want to _____ with you."

The little girl said "Stop! I want to _____ with you."

The horse said "Stop! I want to _____ with you."

The cow said "Stop! I want to _____ with you."

The bird said "Stop! I want to _____ with you."

The frog said "Stop! I want to _____ with you."

trot	fly	moo	play	hop	bake

Illustrations © Theresa Tibbetts/Beehive Illustration.

Dear helper
Objective: To use a familiar story for planning a new story.
Task: Tell the story of 'The Gingerbread Man' to your child and discuss why the fox says something different to the Gingerbread Man. Explain how the story might change and use the above to develop your child's own story. You will find a version of the story at: www.bbc.co.uk/cbeebies/stories/colour/ gingerbreadman.shtml

Name _____   Date _____

Full stop ahead!

- Read the story of Tog.
- Find the full stops and put a ring around each one.

Tog the Dog

One day Tog the Dog went out for a jog.

It was a very wet day and the path

was so muddy he fell into a bog.

Nearby was a big log and he managed

to pull himself out of the bog onto the log.

He was covered in mud and frightened a

frog sat by the bog. He had to jog all

the way home. Finally Tog the Dog reached

home and sat on a log to dry.

Dear helper
Objective: To identify full stops and take account of them when reading.
Task: Read the story of Tog with your child and encourage them to pause where there is a full stop. Ask your child to track carefully through the words and put rings round the full stops. Talk about using full stops to mark the end of sentences and how this helps to read a text and understand its meaning.

Name	Date

Tog the Dog

- Read this story.
- Find the rhyming words.

Have you heard of Tog the Dog?

One day Tog went out for a jog.

He got lost in a fog,

tripped over a cog,

fell into a bog,

and frightened a frog.

Text and illustrations © 1988, Jacqui and Colin Hawkins.

Dear helper
Objective: To read a story independently and to look for rhyming words.
Task: Read the story above with your child and talk about what happens. Then ask your child to try to read it alone. Read it again and ask your child to supply the rhyming words while you pause. You could also highlight all the rhyming words and discuss the shared letter patterns.

Name   Date

Rhyming pairs

cliff	frill	fluff	click
spell	sniff	smell	bring
puff	floss	drill	sprung
cross	speck	trick	mess
dress	spring	fleck	clung

- Cut out the word cards above.

- Jumble them up and lay them face down.

- Take turns to turn a pair over. If you turn over a pair that rhymes, keep it. The player with the most pairs at the end wins.

Dear helper
Objective: To pick out rhyming words and to investigate their spellings.
Task: Help your child to investigate the spellings of the words, pointing out the word endings '-ff', '-ll', '-ss', '-ck' and '-ng'.

| Name | Date |

'Ea' snap

! Tip: Say the words aloud slowly.

head	ear	dead	hear
thread	eat	bread	seat
lead	dear	spread	clear
beach	deaf	reach	steady
team	fear	meal	idea

■ Cut out the cards above.

■ Play 'Snap' by matching the words that have the same **ea** sound.

Illustrations © Pete Smith/Beehive Illustration.

Dear helper
Objective: To be able to match 'ea' words by their sound.
Task: Cut out the cards and shuffle them. Give half the cards to your child and take it in turns to turn a card over. Shout 'Snap' if both words have the same 'ea' sound (either 'ea' as in *head* or 'ea' as in *ear*). If the person who shouts is correct, they keep the cards. The player with the most cards is the winner.

NARRATIVE

Name   Date

Beginnings and endings

■ Read what it says inside each book and decide whether it is a beginning or an ending to a story.

■ Write either **beginning** or **ending** appropriately in the space at the bottom of each book.

When I was five	They all lived happily ever after	A long time ago
They all had tea	Once upon a time	Everyone went home
Then it was time for bed	One day last summer	There was once a monster called Bodrum

Illustrations © Theresa Tibbetts/Beehive Illustration.

Dear helper
Objective: To be able to identify beginnings and endings of stories.
Task: Help your child to read what is in the boxes. Discuss whether they could be a beginning or an ending and relate them to stories they may have read.

Unit 3 📖 **Traditional and fairy tales**

Name	Date

Beginning, middle and ending

- ◼ Cut out the pictures and the words.
- ◼ Match the pictures with the correct speech bubbles.
- ◼ Put them in the correct order to show the beginning, middle and end of the story.

Ow! Ow! Ow! Ow!

Who's going trip-trap, trip-trap over my bridge?

We'd like to eat the grass on the other side of the river.

Illustrations © Theresa Tibbetts/Beehive Illustration.

Dear helper
Objective: To arrange a story in the correct order.
Task: Tell your child the story of 'The Three Billy Goats Gruff' or watch the story at
http://ngfl.northumberland.gov.uk/english/goats/billygoatsgruff.html Help your child arrange the pictures
and appropriate speech bubbles in the correct order.

NARRATIVE

Name   Date

The Three Billy Goats Gruff

■ Ask your helper to read this story with you.

Once upon a time there were three goats: Little Billy Goat Gruff, Big Billy Goat Gruff and Great Big Billy Goat Gruff. They lived in a field, but the goats wanted to eat the grass in another field at the other side of the river. To get to the field they had to cross the bridge, but under the bridge lived a nasty, horrible, goat-eating Troll.

One day Little Billy Goat Gruff felt brave and decided to cross the bridge. So off he trotted, trip-trap, trip-trap over the bridge.

"Who is going trip-trap, trip-trap over my bridge?" roared the Troll.

"Little Billy Goat Gruff," replied the goat.

"Then I will eat you up!" snarled the Troll.

"No! No! Do not eat me! I am too little. Eat Big Billy Goat Gruff when he comes over the bridge. He is much fatter."

"Mmmm, yes, I'd rather have a fatter goat," answered the Troll.

So Little Billy Goat Gruff ran trip-trap, trip-trap over the bridge.

Then Big Billy Goat Gruff went trip-trap, trip-trap over the bridge.

The same thing happened.

"Mmmm, yes, I'd rather have a fatter goat," said the Troll.

So Big Billy Goat Gruff ran trip-trap, trip-trap over the bridge.

At last Great Big Billy Goat Gruff decided to cross the bridge and so off he went, trip-trap, trip-trap over the bridge. Exactly the same thing happened.

"Who is going trip-trap, trip-trap over my bridge?" roared the Troll.

"Great Big Billy Goat Gruff," replied the goat.

"Then I will eat you up!" snarled the Troll, and he jumped onto the bridge.

Great Big Billy Goat Gruff pointed his horns and charged at the Troll. His sharp horns caught the Troll and tossed him into the air, over the bridge and into the deep river.

"Ow! Ow! Ow!" cried the Troll.

"Hee! Hee ! Hee!" laughed the goats, and all three ate the grass on the other side of the river.

■ Now, tell the story to your helper or someone else.

Illustrations © Theresa Tibbetts/Beehive Illustration.

Dear helper
Objective: To retell a story giving the main points in sequence.
Task: Read the story of 'The Three Billy Goats Gruff' with or to your child. Then, ask your child to retell the story back to you, helping them as necessary with prompts to remember the beginning, middle and ending of the story.

Name	Date

The Polar Bear and the Hobyahs

■ Read the story.

■ Then, retell it to your helper, making sure that you remember all that happens in the story.

Once upon a time there was a little old man and a little old woman who lived in a little house in the forest. They were very happy except at Christmas, because every Christmas the Hobyahs came.

The Hobyahs were very naughty, horrible little creatures who ate all the Christmas food, smashed all the Christmas presents and tore up all the Christmas cards every year.

One year, just before Christmas, a great big furry Polar Bear knocked at the door. "Can I come in and stay for Christmas?" he asked. "I'm very lonely and cold," he said. The little old man and the little old woman felt very sorry for him so they let him in.

Then on Christmas Eve the Hobyahs came. They came down the chimney and in through the windows. They screeched and screamed as they ran all over the table and the shelves, smashing jars, eating food, spilling drink and lapping it up. They smashed presents and tore up cards, and then they sat on the Polar Bear because they thought he was a rug.

The Polar Bear did not like what the Hobyahs had done and, most of all, he didn't like them sitting on him. All of a sudden he roared and shook so that the Hobyahs fell on the floor and against the walls. The terrified Hobyahs ran out of the house while the Polar Bear still roared.

When they had all gone, the Polar Bear went over to the cupboard where the little old man and the little old woman were hiding and said, "You can come out now."

The little old woman said, "Thank you" and gave the Polar Bear some warm milk. Then they all worked together to tidy the house and prepare the food for Christmas.

All was quiet and peaceful. As for the Hobyahs they were too frightened ever to return again.

Traditional story

Dear helper
Objective: To retell the story, giving the main points in sequence and to use appropriate expression.
Task: Your child will need help in reading the story, so first read the story to them. Then, read it again with your child joining in, to help them remember the story. Then, listen to your child retell the story.

NARRATIVE

Name   Date

Finger puppets

- Cut out the characters.
- Cut out the strips.
- Stick the strip to the back of the puppet to make a strap for your finger.

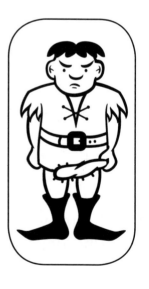 

Dear helper
Objective: To retell the story of 'Jack and the Beanstalk'.
Task: Tell the story of 'Jack and the Beanstalk' to your child and/or watch the story together at: www.bbc.co.uk/cbeebies/stories. Encourage your child to use the finger puppets to tell the story in the correct order using the familiar story language such as *once upon a time* and *Fee, fi, fo, fum*.

Name   Date

Jack and the Beanstalk

◼ Read the play script with expression.

Scene 1

Mother: Jack, I want you to sell Daisy at the market so we can have money to buy food.

Jack: Yes mum.

Mother: Make sure you get a good price for Daisy. She is a good milker and we need the money or we will starve!

Jack: Yes mum, I will.

Scene 2

Man: Hello little boy. Where are you going with your fine cow?

Jack: I am going to the market to sell her so that we can have money to buy food.

Man: I have something much better than money! I will swap these magic beans for your cow.

Jack: Magic beans?

Man: Yes, magic beans!

Jack: But will you look after Daisy?

Man: Oh yes. I love animals.

Jack: That's good. Mum will be pleased.

Illustrations © Theresa Tibbetts/Beehive Illustration.

Dear helper
Objective: To read aloud with expression.
Task: Tell the story of 'Jack and the Beanstalk' to your child and/or watch the story together at: www.bbc.co.uk/cbeebies/stories. Read the play script changing your voice to match the characters and act out the roles with your child to encourage reading with expression.

Name   Date

What happens next?

🔳 Look at the pictures from the 'Three Little Pigs' and
'The Three Billy Goats Gruff' and write about what happens next.

🔳 Write what happens next:

_____

_____

_____

🔳 Write what happens next:

_____

_____

_____

Illustrations © Theresa Tibbetts/Beehive Illustration.

Dear helper
Objective: To retell the story in order to discuss and write about what happens next.
Task: Encourage your child to retell the stories of the two familiar traditional tales. Discuss the part of
the story depicted in the pictures in order to help your child write what happens next.

NARRATIVE

Name   Date

What's happening?

◼ Look at what is happening in the pictures and talk about it with your helper.

◼ Retell the story to your helper.

◼ Write what is happening in the picture in the space underneath each picture.

_____

_____

_____

_____

_____

_____

_____

_____

_____

_____

_____

_____

Illustrations © Theresa Tibbetts/Beehive Illustration.

Dear helper
Objective: To say what is happening in the pictures and to retell the story.
Task: Encourage your child to discuss what is happening in the pictures. Talk about the whole story of 'Cinderella' and help your child to retell it. Support your child by helping them write a sentence about what is happening in each picture.

NARRATIVE

Name _____ Date _____

The Little Red Hen: a picture story

◀ Look at the pictures and tell the story.

Illustrations © Theresa Tibbetts/Beehive Illustration.

Dear helper
Objective: To retell a known story from pictures.
Task: Look carefully with your child at the pictures showing the story of 'The Little Red Hen'. Read the speech bubbles together. Now, ask your child to retell the story, using the pictures as an aid. You could also try cutting up the pictures and seeing if your child can put them back in the correct order.

Name	Date

The Little Red Hen

■ Look at the pictures and write the story. Use the words in the box to help you.

Little Red Hen   help   dog   cat   pig   plant   bake   bread

Who will help me plant this wheat?

Not I.

Once upon a time there was

_____

_____

_____

_____

_____

_____

_____

Who will help me bake this bread?

Not I.

Who will help me eat this bread?

I will.

_____

_____

_____

_____

Illustrations © Theresa Tibbetts/Beehive Illustration.

Dear helper
Objective: To write captions for pictures.
Task: Help your child to write a sentence to fit each picture of the story of 'The Little Red Hen'. You might explain that this represents the beginning, middle and end of the story.

Name _____   Date _____

What's wrong?

■ Read the story and draw a line under all the wrong words.

The Little Red Hen

Once upon a week there was a Little Red Hen who wanted to wheat some plant. She asked the cat, dog and pig to hop. They would not help. So she planted the water and waited for it to grow. She asked the cat, dig and pig to help cut the wheat but they would not hop. She cut it herself. She asked them to help grind the water but they would not hop. So she did it herself. They did not want to help her build the bread so she did it herself. They did want to hop eat the bread, but she did that all by themselves.

Illustrations © Theresa Tibbetts/Beehive Illustration.

Dear helper
Objective: To use knowledge about correct words to check if sentences make sense.
Task: Read the story with your child and see how many mistakes they spot. Re-read the story and ask your child to underline all the incorrect words.

The Clever Cockerel and the Crafty Fox

The following sentences tell the story of a clever cockerel and a crafty fox, but someone has forgotten to include the capital letters and the full stops.

■ Put capital letters and full stops where you think they should go.

one day a crafty fox had a plan to catch a clever cockerel

the fox was always thinking of plans to catch the cockerel but he hadn't managed it yet

the crafty fox went to the barn where the cockerel lived

the crafty fox tricked the cockerel and threw a sack over the cockerel's head

the fox ran off as fast as he could with the sack over his shoulder

the clever cockerel took a pair of scissors out of his waistcoat pocket and cut a hole big enough for him to get through

quick as a wink the cockerel put a stone as heavy as himself into the sack and ran as fast as he could back to his barn

soon the fox arrived at his den and emptied out the sack over a pot of boiling water

the stone crashed into the pot and the boiling water splashed all over the silly fox

the clever cockerel laughed when he heard the silly fox yell

■ Now read the story with your helper.

Illustrations © Theresa Tibbetts/Beehive Illustration.

Dear helper
Objective: To use capital letters and full stops correctly.
Task: Help your child to read the sentences and discuss where to put capital letters and full stops. Then, read the whole story through together.

Name   Date

Ooh, look at that!

- Look at the words in the list. They all contain **oo**.
  - ☐ In some of the words the **oo** makes a sound like the **oo** in f**oo**d.
  - ☐ In others the **oo** makes a sound like the **oo** in g**oo**d.
- Sort the words out and write them underneath **good** or **food** to show how they should be pronounced.

moon	fool	blood	soon	soot
shoot	room	stood	foot	cool
zoo	look	wool	roof	spoon
cook	tooth	mood	tool	hook
book	wood	broom	hood	crook

good	food

Dear helper

Objective: To revise reading and spelling of words which contain /oo/ as in *food* and /oo/ as in *good*.
Task: Read the words with your child and talk about the two main different sounds that can be made using 'oo'. Help your child to sort the words. If necessary, say the words aloud, exaggerating the 'oo' sound.

Name	Date

Phoneme sounds (1)

■ Say each sound you hear in the following words.

■ Use a pencil to draw a line between the sounds.

s / p / o o / n

spoon	moon	root
oat	goat	boat
train	rain	drain
meet	street	fleet
tie	pie	lie

Dear helper

Objective: To identify the separate sounds in words to make spelling them easier.

Task: A phoneme is the smallest unit of sound in a word. Help your child to distinguish the vowel sound made up of two letters in the words above. Drawing a pencil line between each sound will help your child to distinguish the individual letter sounds and the single vowel sound made by the two vowel letters.

Long vowel sounds (1)

■ Read aloud the words in the grid.

  ❑ Cover **y** words with a blue counter.

  ❑ Cover **igh** words with a red counter.

  ❑ Cover **ie** words with a green counter.

why	spy	sigh	by
cry	lie	try	nigh
high	my	dry	fry
pie	shy	tie	sly

■ How many different spellings can you find for the sound **ie** as in **pie**?

■ Use some of the words to make sentences.

■ Write your sentences here:

1. _____

2. _____

3. _____

4. _____

5. _____

Dear helper

Objective: To recognise some of the common spelling patterns for the long vowel sound 'ie'. (The short vowel sound would be /i/ as in *pig* but the long vowel sound would be /ie/ as in *pie*).

Task: Help your child to carry out the task and discuss the different spelling patterns 'y', 'ie', and 'igh'. Use different coins or dried beans if you don't have counters. Then, encourage your child to use some of the words in sentences. If necessary, give help with writing the sentences.

Name	Date

Slime World

- Look at the picture of Slime World.

- What do you notice?

- What do you think is different about Slime World and our world?

Illustrations © Theresa Tibbetts/Beehive Illustration.

Dear helper

Objective: To encourage discussion about how a fantasy setting differs from our world.

Task: Your child will have been working with other children to talk about how fantasy worlds differ from their own. Help your child to discuss with you the detail in the picture of Slime World so that similarities and differences with our world are explored.

NARRATIVE

Name	Date

Book covers

■ Look at these book covers. What do you think the stories will be about? Talk about them with your helper.

Illustrations © Theresa Tibbetts/Beehive Illustration.

Dear helper
Objective: To predict what a story will be about from the book cover and to discuss preferences and give reasons.
Task: Discuss with your child what is being portrayed on the book covers and ask which books they would prefer to read and why. Share your own ideas and preferences as well.

Name   Date

What sort of story?

◼ Read the blurbs on the backs of the books and discuss with your helper what you think the stories will be about.

The alien zoo needs a new creature to keep the head keeper happy. So an expedition is mounted to find the creature with the most heads in the universe. If the explorers do not find this amazing creature they will be thrown into the head keeper's pet food bowl!

Daisy and Lucy are friends but when Daisy takes a ride on a mysterious new girl's flying bicycle and visits strange and wonderful places, her friendship with Lucy becomes threatened.

Charlie is in a hurry to tell his mum about his part in a school play, but on the way home he meets some strange creatures.

The Slimers' world is threatened by global cooling such that their slithering days appear numbered as they will soon be frozen to the spot. What can they do to warm up their freezing world and return to their happy days of sliming around?

Illustrations © Theresa Tibbetts/Beehive Illustration.

Dear helper
Objective: To use book 'blurbs' to predict the content of stories.
Task: Help your child to read the book blurbs, one at a time, and discuss what the story might be about.

NARRATIVE

Name	Date

Tell your fantasy story

■ Cut out the pictures.

■ Choose the pictures you want to use that will help you to tell a story.

Illustrations © Theresa Tibbetts/Beehive Illustration.

Dear helper
Objective: To create a story to tell.
Task: Talk to your child about the scenes and characters in the pictures. Ask your child to choose pictures and help your child to make up a story and tell it to you.

PHOTOCOPIABLE 📖 **SCHOLASTIC**
www.scholastic.co.uk

Name   Date

Robot 144

■ Ask your helper to read the story to you.

■ Retell the story.

Robot 144 was watching the planet's two suns set one after the other in the copper-coloured sky having plugged himself into his night charging socket. This was his usual routine after his day's work in the Robot repair factory.

Something in the sky this night was different, causing his standby circuit to switch to active mode. He did not like the tingling feeling in his circuits. He knew he should be resting in this time phase.

His computer brain started to work on what his camera eyes had seen, again causing more tingling in his circuits. Now he really was concerned. He liked everything to follow his daily programme. Why was his routine being disturbed?

He had a read-out from his computer. At the top it said YOUR PLANET IS BEING INVADED. Immediately his eyes started to flash on and off and his communication system produced a terrifying siren wail. Suddenly from all around his fellow robots emerged from their recharging centres. Robot 144 had already beamed his report to computer central so all the other robots accessed the news.

From 144's report they learned that in the night an alien spaceship had approached their planet. This alien ship possessed a huge magnet which had already captured many robots simply by picking them up from the planet's surface and capturing them with a CLANG on its magnet.

The situation was clear. The aliens would strip the planet of all its robots and, according to a message from the alien ship, take the robots as robot slaves back to the alien home planet far off in another galaxy.

What could be done? Within seconds the answer was flashed to them by the central computer. They all returned to their charging points. They plugged in and central computer's circuits switched on the chargers. The robots, in contact with the planet's metal surface, vibrated with energy as the whole planet became one huge magnet. This had a dramatic effect! Robot 144's camera eyes told his computer brain that the alien spaceship's magnet was repelled by the planet's magnetic force and the alien spaceship was shot off into outer space! The robots were saved!

Dear helper
Objective: To retell a story with support.
Task: Read the story to your child, embellishing the action and discussing the events with your child to help create visual imagery. Help your child to retell the story to you.

NARRATIVE

Name

Date

Roto and the Hullaloobs

- Read this extract with your helper.

- Talk to your helper about the characters.

Roto dashed into the cave for safety. All he could hear was himself ticking furiously as he tried to recover from the chase. As his systems recovered and his sensitizer adjusted to the darkness he registered another creature in the cave on his head screen. The creature was registering as warmer than he was, definitely more mobile, and noisier.

"Who are you?" asked Roto mechanically.

"Hullaloo." came the reply. "I am Hullaloo, king of the Hullaloobs."

"There is another creature. Who is the other creature?"

"Hullalee, queen of the Hullaloobs." came the reply. "Who is chasing you?"

"A Clawker is chasing me."

In a frightened voice queen Hullalee replied that they too were being pursued by the Clawkers.

"There is very little time. We have no time." said Roto.

At which point several Clawkers slammed on their claw brakes forming a tight clawing line across the cave entrance. All three were trapped!

Dear helper

Objective: To describe the characters in the extract.

Task: Read the extract to your child. Discuss what is happening and ask questions that will help your child to describe the characters. Possible questions might be: *Are there any clues in the text to suggest what Roto might look like? Do you think that Hullaloo and Hullalee are mechanical? Why or why not? What do you know about the Clawkers? What might they look like? Who might be the hero or heroine of the story and can you suggest why? Do you think that the Clawkers are dangerous? Can you say why?*

Name	Date

Illustrations © Theresa Tibbetts/Beehive Illustration.

Storyline

■ Cut out the pictures and stick them in the correct places on the storyline.

Storyline

problem	afraid	resolution	happy ending

Dear helper
Objective: To understand that stories are often structured around a problem and its resolution.
Task: Help your child to put the pictures in the correct places on the storyline. Talk about how the story involves a problem that is resolved happily.

Name   Date

Phoneme sounds (2)

■ Say each sound you hear in the following words.
■ Use a pencil to draw a line between the sounds.

b / l / ue   b / oo / k

week   plain   bloat

fly   true   flew

show   shoe   book

cheese   bloom   tight

spoon   crown   bright

Illustrations © Theresa Tibbetts/Beehive Illustration.

Dear helper
Objective: To identify the separate sounds in words to make spelling them easier.
Task: A phoneme is the smallest unit of sound in a word. Help your child to distinguish the sounds in each word. Drawing a pencil line between each sound will help your child to distinguish the sounds.

Name	Date

Long vowel sounds (2)

■ Read aloud the words in the grid.

☐ Cover **o** words with a blue counter.

☐ Cover **oe** words with a red counter.

☐ Cover **ow** words with a green counter.

toe	row	go	snow
no	woe	crow	bow
slow	grow	foe	throw
hoe	show	so	low

■ How many different spellings can you find for the sound **ow** as in **low**?

■ Use some of the words to make sentences.

■ Write your sentences here:

1. _____

2. _____

3. _____

4. _____

5. _____

Illustrations © Theresa Tibbetts/Beehive Illustration.

Dear helper
Objective: To recognise some of the common spelling patterns for the long vowel sound /oe/.
(The short vowel sound would be /o/ as in *cot* but the long vowel sound would be /oe/ as in *toe*).
Task: Help your child to carry out the task and discuss the different spelling patterns 'o', 'oe', and 'ow'. Use different coins or dried beans if you don't have counters. Then, encourage your child to use some of the words in sentences. If necessary, give help with writing the sentences.

CORE SKILLS

Spelling game

after	again	all	and	away
but	came	can	come	could
don't	for	from	go	had
just	like	me	my	not
now	once	over	people	see
so	them	they	time	to
too	very	was	were	where
who	with	would	yellow	you

- Cut out the words to make 40 individual cards.
- Spread them out with the words face down.
- Take turns with another player to pick up a word and to say the word out loud. Don't show the word to the other player.
- If the other player can write the word down correctly, they keep the card. Check the spelling by looking at the card. If the word is not spelled correctly, put the card back, face down.
- The player who has the most cards when all of them have been picked up is the winner.

Illustrations © Pete Smith/Beehive Illustration.

Dear helper
Objective: To be able to spell common words.
Task: You may wish to play the game with a reduced number of cards. Make sure that there are plenty of words that your child can spell easily as well as a few that are more challenging. Add new words if your child is able to spell all of the words.

Name	Date

How would you feel?

◾ How would you feel in these situations?

◾ Look at each picture and write a sentence under each one to describe your feelings.

Illustrations © Theresa Tibbetts/Beehive Illustration.

Dear helper

Objective: To write in sentences using capital letters and full stops correctly.

Task: Discuss each picture with your child, asking them how they would feel in the same situation, and perhaps offering an idea of how you would feel. Then, help them to compose a sentence or two for each picture that describes their feelings.

Name   Date

Label the house

- The following words describe parts of a house.

  door   tiles   window   roof
  gutter   bricks   chimney   drainpipe

- Use them to help you write labels for the picture.

- Draw a line from the part of the house to the label like the one that is already done for you.

gutter

Dear helper
Objective: To label a picture.
Task: Help your child to read the words in order to label correctly the parts of the house.

PHOTOCOPIABLE   ■SCHOLASTIC
www.scholastic.co.uk

Name   Date

Can you help?

◼ Look at the pictures and finish the captions.

I help my friend _____

_____

_____

I help my teacher _____

_____

_____

I help my mum _____

_____

_____

I help my dad _____

_____

_____

Illustrations © Theresa Tibbetts/Beehive Illustration.

NON-FICTION

Dear helper
Objective: To write captions to fit pictures.
Task: Look carefully at each picture with your child. Talk about what is happening and help them to write a sentence to fit.

The garden centre

- Add capital letters and full stops to the captions in the boxes.
- Cut out and match the completed sentences to the pictures.

CORE SKILLS

	cacti do not need much water
	the sunflower likes full sunshine
 HALF PRICE!	bunches of holly make colourful Christmas decorations
	bush apple trees are ideal for patio planting
	watering cans are on special offer today

Illustrations © Theresa Tibbetts/Beehive Illustration.

Dear helper
Objective: To write a caption for a picture in a complete sentence with a capital letter and full stop.
Task: Point out to your child that something is missing from the captions. Ask what you need to change, and what do you need to add, for it to become a complete sentence. Help your child to put the capital letters and full stops in the right place. Then match corrected captions to the pictures.

Name	Date

Instruction language

■ Pick out the instructions and highlight them.

This way to the flower garden
⟶

The flower gardens are very beautiful, especially in spring.

The teacher said that the glue took a long time to dry

Whisk 2 eggs

Mummy and Daddy always tell me not to touch plugs

Many plants need full sunshine to grow well

Plant sunflowers in a sunny place

Glue the 2 pieces together to make a corner

DO NOT TOUCH!

Dear helper
Objective: To identify instructions.
Task: Tell your child that some of the boxes are instructions and some are not. Help your child to pick out the instructions by discussing what instructions contain, such as 'doing words' like *plant*, *whisk* and *glue* and their factual structure such as their need for numbers.

NON-FICTION

Name	Date

NON-FICTION

How to make a jungle scene

■ Read the instructions below and make the jungle scene.

You will need:
- ☐ Background picture
- ☐ Animal pictures
- ☐ Crayons
- ☐ Scissors
- ☐ Glue

1. Colour the background of the jungle.
2. Colour the animals carefully.
3. Cut out the animals.
4. Stick the animals carefully on the picture.
5. Admire your picture!

Illustrations © Theresa Tibbetts/Beehive Illustration.

Dear helper
Objective: To read and follow simple instructions.
Task: Read these instructions with your child. Make sure you have the necessary equipment and then help your child to read and follow each instruction carefully. Take the finished picture to school to show the teacher.

Name	Date

How to make a fruit salad

- The pictures below show how to make a fruit salad.

- Write a simple explanation underneath each picture. Say what is happening. Some words are given to help you.

Cut _____ Peel _____

_____ _____

Slice _____ Squeeze _____

_____ _____

Illustrations © Theresa Tibbetts/Beehive Illustration.

NON-FICTION

Dear helper
Objective: To write simple instructions.
Task: Explain to your child that what is written should explain what is happening in the picture, for example: *Cut the apple.* They should end up with a recipe for making fruit salad in words and pictures.

My jungle scene

- Look at your jungle scene picture.
- Now write some sentences to describe it.

The tiger looks at _____

_____

The snake hisses at _____

_____

The monkey climbs the _____

_____

The parrot's feathers are _____

_____

Words to help

trees	elephant	monkey	green
tiger	snake	red	yellow
parrot	small	blue	big

Illustrations © Theresa Tibbetts/Beehive Illustration.

Dear helper
Objective: To write a caption.
Task: Your child should look carefully at the picture of the jungle that they have constructed previously for homework. They should now complete the sentences above to describe it. They can use the words above to help them. Encourage your child to write more sentences if they are able.

Change the word

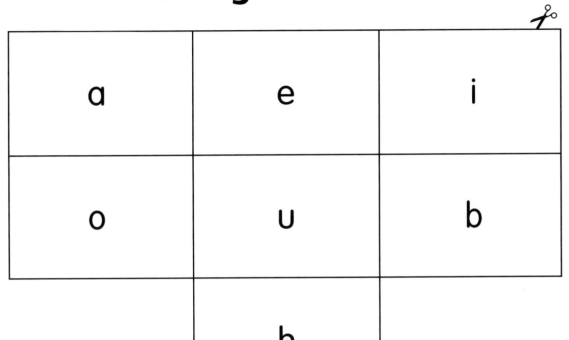

- Cut out the letters above.
- Place the vowels (**a**, **e**, **i**, **o** and **u**) in turn into the space between **p** and **t** below.
- How many words can you make?
- Now place the **b** over the **p** and play the game again.
- Play it again using the **h** instead of the **p**.

p		t

Dear helper

Objective: To blend three letters to read a word.

Task: This is a game, where you need to cut out the vowel letters ('a', 'e', 'i', 'o', 'u') and ask your child to place one letter at a time in between the 'p' and 't' to see which words they can make. Say the words each time with your child and encourage them to write a list of the words they make. The letters 'b' and 'h' have also been included for you to substitute with 'p' to make further words.

CORE SKILLS

Blend a word

- Your helper will cover the first letter.
- Read the word.
- Then read the word with the first letter uncovered.

spot   spit   gran

spin   crib   slid

stop   cram   flap

glad

Dear helper
Objective: To reinforce phonics for spelling.
Task: Cover the first letters in the words above with a strip of card. With your child read the word remaining, for example pot, then lower the strip of card to reveal the 's' and read together the new word spot. Repeat this for all the words.

Name	Date

School day (1)

◾ Look at the pictures and read the captions.

 The whistle was blown at 9 o'clock.	 The teacher called the register at half past nine.
 We had assembly at 10 o'clock.	 We had our dinner at 12 o'clock.
 We had playtime at 2 o'clock.	 At 3 o'clock it was time to go home.

◾ Answer the following questions:

　1. What time was assembly?

　2. What happened at 12 o'clock?

◾ Talk about the children's day at school using the words in the box.

first	then	next	later	afterwards

NON-FICTION

Illustrations © Theresa Tibbetts/Beehive Illustration.

Dear helper

Objective: To read captions, answer questions and retell a narrative.

Task: Look carefully at the pictures above and read the captions with your child. Help them to answer the questions and talk about what happens using the connective words. Discuss with your child how their school day is different to that described.

Name   Date

School day (2)

■ Match the words to the pictures by writing the correct number under each picture.

1. First the teacher called the register.

2. Then we lined up for assembly.

3. Next we all joined in with singing.

4. Later we held up number cards in maths.

5. Afterwards we read with our teacher.

6. Finally we listened to a story before we went home.

NON-FICTION

Illustrations © Theresa Tibbetts/Beehive Illustration.

Dear helper
Objective: To match captions to pictures.
Task: Ask your child to read each caption and help if necessary. Then, match the captions to the appropriate pictures, putting a number underneath each picture.

Name	Date

My day at school

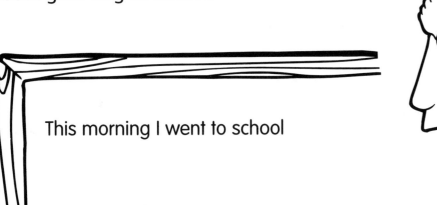

Use the writing frame to help you write about your day at school.

This morning I went to school

To begin with

Next I

Then

After that

Finally I

Now

Dear helper
Objective: To be able to write an ordered sequence of events about the school day.
Task: Discuss with your child the things that have happened at school. Then, using the writing frame, help your child to write about them in the sequence in which they occurred.

NON-FICTION

Name	Date

Indexes

- These two non-fiction books need indexes.
- Sort the words and write them in alphabetical order to make an index for each book. List the words, putting their page number next to them.

All About Seeds

seeds	1
dandelions	5
conkers	4
wind	5
keys	4
burrs	4
nuts	3
pips	2

Index		page
burrs		4
conkers		4
_____		
_____		
_____		
_____		
_____		

Life Cycle of a Butterfly

eggs	2
caterpillar	2
butterfly	1
pupae	3
wings	4
flowers	2
nectar	5
leaves	2

Index		page
butterfly		1
caterpillar		2
_____		
_____		
_____		
_____		
_____		

NON-FICTION

Illustrations © Theresa Tibbetts/Beehive Illustration.

Dear helper
Objective: To sort a jumbled list of words into alphabetical order for an index.
Task: Help your child to read the words in the lists. Discuss how to order the words into alphabetical order, and ask questions, for example: *Which word should come first? Why?* Look at some books at home that have indexes.

Name   Date

Using dictionaries

■ Arrange the following words in alphabetical order.

■ Look up their meaning in a dictionary.

first   laugh   again   water

_____

_____

_____

_____

■ Write a sentence for each word.

■ Write your sentences here:

1. _____

_____

2. _____

_____

3. _____

_____

4. _____

_____

Illustrations © Theresa Tibbetts/Beehive Illustration.

NON-FICTION

Dear helper
Objective: To be able to use a simple dictionary and to understand its alphabetical organisation.
Task: Discuss the way a dictionary is organised in alphabetical order. Help your child to find the words in the dictionary, read their meaning and write a simple sentence for each word to show they understand the meaning.

Extend a word

- Your helper will cover the last letter.
- Read the word.
- Then read the word with the last letter uncovered.

tent   hump   sump

bend   pant   damp

mend   tint   ramp

rump

Dear helper
Objective: To reinforce phonics for spelling.
Task: Cover the last letters with a strip of card. With your child read the word remaining for example
ten, then lower the strip of card to reveal the 't' and read together the new word *tent*. Repeat this for all
the words.

Name	Date

Question or not?

- Read the following sentences.
- Put a question mark at the end of the sentence if you think it is a question and a full stop at the end of those which are not.

Monkeys are mischievous

Are monkeys mischievous

What do pandas eat

Pandas eat bamboo plants

A tiger's coat is yellow and black striped

What colour is a tiger's coat

Polar bears can catch fish to eat

What do polar bears eat

Where do giraffes live

Giraffes live in Africa

Illustrations © Theresa Tibbetts/Beehive Illustration.

Dear helper
Objective: To be able to identify questions and use the question mark appropriately.
Task: Help your child to read each sentence and decide whether it is a question or not. You could help your child by reading the sentences aloud, using the expression and inflection appropriate to the ones that are questions.

Name   Date

Ask a question

◼ Write five questions you would like answered about the duck. Use the **question words** to start your questions.

An example could be: Where do ducks sleep?

Don't forget the question mark!

1. Where _____

2. What _____

3. When _____

4. How _____

5. Why _____

Illustrations © Theresa Tibbetts/Beehive Illustration.

Dear helper
Objective: To be able to write questions.
Task: Talk to your child about the duck in the picture and raise questions together. It is important for your child to be able to ask questions so they can look for their answers when reading. The question words *where, what, when, how* and *why* will help them to do this.

NON-FICTION

Name	Date

Questions, questions

◂ Look at the picture.

◂ Write five questions you could ask someone about the picture.

◂ Write your questions here:

1. Where _____

2. What _____

3. When _____

4. How _____

5. Why _____

NON-FICTION

Dear helper
Objective: To write simple questions.
Task: Discuss the picture with your child and help to raise questions. Assist your child in writing some of the questions, for example: *What shop is next to the butcher's? How many children are on scooters?*

Name   Date

All about seeds

■ Read 'All about seeds' with your helper.

All about seeds

Most plants make seeds in order to make new plants. The plant forms seeds when its flowers stop blooming. Sometimes you can see the old flower at the end of a pea pod or at the end of a rose hip. In a pea pod the seeds are in a row inside the pod and we like eating them. In a rose hip the seeds are very tiny. We don't eat those seeds, but we can eat the covering called the hip when it is made into rose hip syrup. We eat lots of seeds such as lentils, beans, peanuts, and pumpkin and sunflower seeds that we can roast and scatter on bread. The coconut is one of the biggest seeds that grow. We also like to eat the fruit and vegetable coverings that protect seeds, such as melon, pumpkin, apple, peach, orange, cucumber, tomato, cherries, and lots more.

■ Now answer these questions. Write in sentences.

1. Why do plants make seeds?

Plants make seeds _____ .

2. When do the seeds start to form?

Seeds start to form when _____ .

3. How are the peas arranged in the pod?

Peas are arranged in _____ .

4. Which is one of the biggest seeds that grow?

The _____ is one of the biggest seeds that grow.

5. Which part of the cherry do you think will grow into a new plant?

I think the _____ will grow into a new plant.

Illustrations © Theresa Tibbetts/Beehive Illustration.

Dear helper
Objective: To read and understand non-fiction.
Task: Read or help your child to read the text. Talk about it. Ask: *Is it a story or is it factual? What is it telling us about?* Assist your child in completing the answers to the questions, supporting them by re-reading relevant bits of the text.

NON-FICTION

Name	Date

Favourite animals

The chart shows how some school children recorded a vote for their favourite animal.

			Yvonne	
			Kerry	Marie
Arthur			Robert	John
Joe	Tony	Angela	Katie	James
Sarah	Sam	Gemma	David	Sasha
polar bear	**monkey**	**tiger**	**panda**	**giraffe**

◼ Use the chart to help you answer the questions below. Part of the answer is written for you. Fill in the rest.

1. Which animal does Sam like the best?

Sam likes _____ the best.

2. How many children like monkeys the best?

_____ children like monkeys the best.

3. Which animal is the most popular?

_____ is the most popular animal.

4. How many children voted altogether?

Altogether _____ children voted.

5. Who liked the polar bear the best?

_____ polar bears the best.

6. Which two animals got the same vote?

_____ and _____ got the same vote.

Dear helper
Objective: To be able to locate information on the chart in order to answer questions.
Task: Support your child by helping them to read the questions and locate the information in order to write the answers.

Illustrations © Theresa Tibbetts/Beehive Illustration.

NON-FICTION

Name   Date

My dad

- ◼ Look at this chart about dads.
- ◼ Use it to help you complete the sentences.

children's names	Gemma	Zoran	Fredrick	Natasha	Tim
What is dad's job?	engineer	looks after children	drives a lorry	works at the computer	looks after the house and children
Where does he work?	office	school	on the roads	at home	at home
What does he like doing?	bird watching	golf	fishing	walking	playing basketball
What is his favourite food?	lasagne	chicken chow mein	spare ribs	salmon	strawberries
What is he called?	Jim	Boris	Tony	Josh	Jeremy

1. Zoran's dad looks after _____ in _____.

2. The dad who likes strawberries is called _____.

3. Natasha's dad works at the _____ and likes

   _____ and eating _____.

4. Tim's dad looks after _____ at _____.

   He likes playing _____ and eating _____.

5. Jeremy is _____ dad. He works at _____.

6. Golf is the favourite thing that _____'s dad likes doing.

7. Lasagne is _____ favourite food.

8. Tony drives _____ and is _____ dad.

Dear helper
Objective: To locate information on a chart.
Task: Help your child to locate the information on the chart in order to complete the sentences.

Illustrations © Theresa Tibbetts/Beehive Illustration.

PHOTOCOPIABLE ◣SCHOLASTIC
www.scholastic.co.uk

Name   Date

Fiction or non-fiction?

◼ Look at the book covers. Are they fiction or non-fiction?

◼ Write **fiction** below the books you think are fiction. Write **non-fiction** below the books you think are non-fiction. Could some be both?

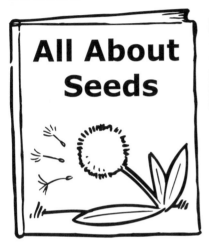

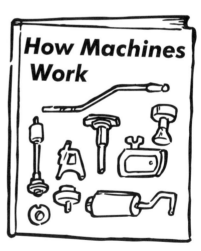

Dear helper
Objective: To understand and use the terms 'fiction' and 'non-fiction' and to predict what a book might be about from its cover.
Task: Make sure your child understands that *fiction* is made up, whereas *non-fiction* is fact. Help your child to talk about and explain the decisions they make about whether the books are fiction or non-fiction.

Name	Date

What I know about my mum

◢ Write eight things you know about your mum, for example:

☐ What does she like?   ☐ What doesn't she like?

☐ What's her favourite sport?   ☐ What's her favourite food?

☐ What makes her so special?

Examples might be: Mum likes football. She's kind.

◢ Then draw a picture of your mum in the frame.

Illustrations © Theresa Tibbetts/Beehive Illustration.

Dear helper
Objective: To use the language and features of information text by providing short phrases or sentences to accompany a picture.
Task: This is an opportunity for your child to talk freely and with confidence about someone who they know best. Help your child to capture the knowledge and thoughts they have about their mum in short phrases or sentences written around the picture.

Name	Date

What is Dad thinking?

◗ The picture shows some of the things Dad likes doing.

◗ Write five sentences describing what he likes. Use the pictures to help you.

◗ Write your sentences here:

_____

_____

_____

_____

_____

Illustrations © Theresa Tibbetts/Beehive Illustration.

Dear helper
Objective: To use information from the pictures to write in sentences to describe what Dad is thinking.
Task: Talk to your child about the things Dad is thinking as he irons, and help your child to write five sentences about Dad's thoughts. It is important that your child does not associate one line with one sentence.

Name   Date

Crocodiles

■ Read about crocodiles with your helper.

■ Discuss and decide on a subheading for each of the two paragraphs.

Crocodiles

The crocodile hides in rivers and lakes and looks for something to eat. Crocodiles can eat frogs and fish whole and they catch larger animals by gripping them in their teeth and spinning round with them. They sometimes eat humans.

Female crocodiles lay eggs which they look after until they hatch. Tiny baby crocodiles listen for their mother's footsteps and call to her. She gently gathers them into her mouth and carries them to the safety of the water.

Illustrations © Theresa Tibbetts/Beehive Illustration.

Dear helper
Objective: To discuss suitable subheadings for the information about crocodiles.
Task: Read the extract about crocodiles to your child and explain that it is giving them information about crocodiles (non-fiction). Talk about the information in each paragraph and help your child to think about a suitable subheading so that it informs you what is in the paragraphs.

PHOTOCOPIABLE ▬SCHOLASTIC
www.scholastic.co.uk

Sentences to punctuate

■ Punctuate the following sentences using capital letters, full stops and question marks correctly. The first one has been done for you.

where were charlotte and emily going
Where were Charlotte and Emily going?

they were going to the fair

_____

what can you do at a fair

_____

charlotte can throw hoops

_____

emily can roll pennies

_____

why does charlotte want to throw hoops

_____

charlotte wants to win a furry teddy

_____

why does emily want to roll pennies

_____

emily wants to win a goldfish

_____

what else can you do at the fair

_____

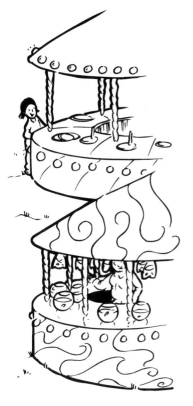

CORE SKILLS

Dear helper
Objective: To punctuate sentences appropriately.
Task: Help your child to read the sentences. Use the word _sentence_ when talking about how to punctuate it correctly. When the task is complete, ask your child to read the sentences aloud using expression appropriate to the grammar, for example raising the voice for questions.

Capital letters

■ Rewrite the sentences with capital letters in the correct places.

mr and mrs bean are welcome to visit
the school on thursday 17th of june.

at assembly on wednesday christine smedley
read the poem a red, red rose by robert burns.

several children chose books by jill murphy
to take home to read.

a favourite children's book is dogger
by shirley hughes.

■ Write your sentences here:

_____

_____

_____

_____

_____

_____

_____

Illustrations © Theresa Tibbetts/Beehive Illustration.

Dear helper
Objective: To use capital letters appropriately.
Task: Help your child to read the sentences, making decisions together about where to put capital letters. Encourage and support your child in writing the sentences with the capital letters in the correct place. They should continue on the back of the sheet if they need more room. Talk about what capital letters are used for: beginning of sentences, names, titles, days of the week, months and so on.

Charlotte, Charles and Chloe

The names below begin with **ch**, but **ch** has a different sound in each.

Charlotte   Charles   Chloe

◼ Read the sentences below and underline the words that have **ch** in them.

1. Whenever Grandad asks me what I would like from the sweet shop, I always choose chocolate.

2. The chef wore a tall, white hat and an apron when he chopped the onions and sliced the cheese.

3. Father Christmas is a jolly character with a beard covering his chin.

4. The choir sang the Christmas carol Chloe chose.

5. Charlie's chum Chris was a cheerful chap.

◼ Write the words that you underlined into this table. Do the words have the same **ch** sound as Charles, Charlotte or Chloe?

Charles	Charlotte	Chloe

Illustrations © Pete Smith/Beehive Illustration.

CORE SKILLS

Dear helper
Objective: To read and spell words beginning with the letters 'ch'.
Task: Read the sentences with your child. Help your child to distinguish between the different sounds that 'ch' can represent and assist them in writing the 'ch' words under the appropriate name.

Chef's chocolate

■ Look at the words in the list. Read them carefully and then decide which **ch** sound they each have and write them next to the correct picture. One has been done for you.

chat	chip	choice	parachute
chrome	chase	child	chair
Christopher	chin	choir	chart
each	ache	machine	Michelle
chef	cherry	Christmas	anchor

chat

chocolate

chef

chemist

■ Add some more **ch** words to the pictures. You could use a dictionary to help you to find more words.

Illustrations © Pete Smith/Beehive Illustration.

Dear helper
Objective: To read and spell words containing the letters 'ch'.
Task: Look at the words that include 'ch' and say them with your child. Next look at the words *chocolate*, *chef* and *chemist* under the pictures. Talk about the different sounds that 'ch' can make. Now help your child to list each of the 'ch' words next to the picture that has the same 'ch' sound. If your child finishes the task easily, try adding some more words. You could look in a dictionary together or in your child's reading book. Talk about which sound for 'ch' seems to be the most common.

Name	Date

Sequence

✂

Next you brush your teeth.
Now you go to bed.
To begin with you put toothpaste on your toothbrush.
After that you rinse your brush.
Finally you put the top back on the toothpaste.
Then you rinse your mouth with water.

◀ Cut out the sentences.

◀ Paste them onto a separate sheet in the correct order.

Illustrations © Theresa Tibbetts/Beehive Illustration.

NON-FICTION

Dear helper

Objective: To re-order the sentences into the correct sequence.

Task: Discuss with your child what you do when you brush your teeth. Talk about the order in which you do things, then read the sentences and help your child to sequence them into the correct order.

Name   Date

Growing plants from seeds

- ◾ Cut out the pictures.
- ◾ Re-order the pictures in the correct sequence and explain what is happening to your helper.

Illustrations © Theresa Tibbetts/Beehive Illustration.

Dear helper
Objective: To sequence pictures in the correct order and explain what is happening.
Task: Discuss each picture in detail with your child and encourage your child to place the pictures in the correct sequence and give you an explanation for their choice.

Name	Date

Getting dressed

◼ Dress the child in the picture as if it was you.

◼ Choose the order in which you put on your clothes.

◼ Tell your helper what you did. Choose words from those given at the bottom of the page to start your sentences.

◼ Write a recount of what you did using the words from the box.

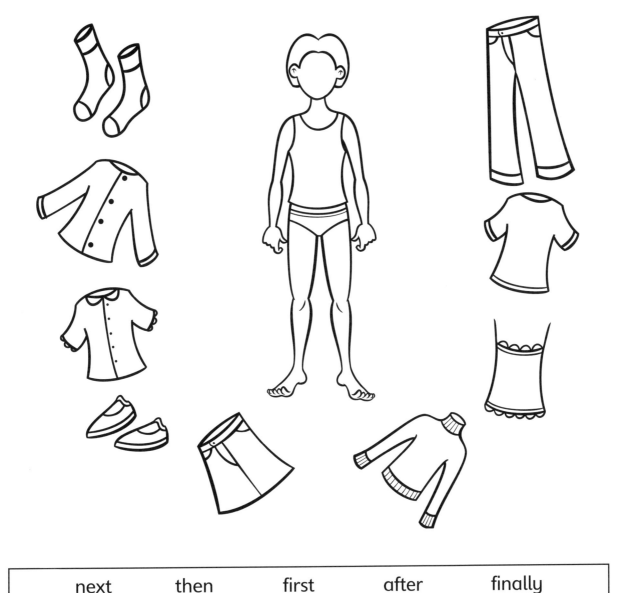

Illustrations © Theresa Tibbetts/Beehive Illustration.

next	then	first	after	finally

NON-FICTION

Dear helper
Objective: To write about a sequence of events using appropriate time connectives.
Task: Use the activity to recount the order in which your child gets dressed. Help your child to write the order in which they get dressed using the words from the selection in the activity to start the sentences.

Name

Date

NON-FICTION

What happens when?

■ Watch the clip 'Growing plants' with your helper.

■ Use the sentence starters to sequence what happens to the seedling when it is watered.

When I start watering the seedling

_____

_____

_____

When I water it again

_____

_____

_____

In the third week

_____

_____

_____

Finally in week four

_____

_____

_____

Dear helper
Objective: To write a recount about what happens to a seedling when it is watered.
Task: Use the online text www.bbc.co.uk/schools/scienceclips/ages/5_6/growing_plants.shtml
View 'Growing plants' several times with your child and discuss in detail what is happening to the seedling when it is watered week by week. Use the sentence starters in the activity to help your child complete a sequence of sentences that describes what is happening to the seedling.

Matching sounds

◼ Underline the words which have the same sound as the bold part of the word on the left. The first one has been done for you.

town Mum's new car was **brown** with grey seats.

g**oo**d It was raining so I covered my head with the hood of my coat.

d**ar**k It was so busy in Hull that we could not find anywhere to park the car.

t**oy** Boys and girls played together happily.

n**ow** The town was full of people.

c**ow** David frowned as he looked at the page of sums.

c**ar**d The sums were too hard for David.

oil The snake coiled itself around the tree.

out There were about twenty people on the bus.

Illustrations © Pete Smith/Beehive Illustration.

CORE SKILLS

Dear helper
Objective: To identify words that have the same vowel sounds and to recognise the common spelling patterns for /oo/, /ar/, /oy/ and /ow/.
Task: Look at the words on the left of the sentences together and say them aloud before trying to find words with the same vowel sound in the sentences. Draw your child's attention to the similar spelling patterns, for example *town, brown; good, hood; toy, boys.*

Odd one out

■ Which word in each row is the odd one out, because it has a different sound highlighted? Put a ring round it.

g**oo**d	w**oo**d	**oi**l
owl	p**ar**t	n**ow**
cl**ow**n	**ou**t	c**oi**n
s**oo**t	f**oo**d	c**oo**k
b**ar**	c**ow**	**ar**t

t**oi**let	b**oy**	h**ow**	c**oi**n
b**oo**k	w**oo**l	p**oo**l	l**oo**k
d**ow**n	b**oo**t	t**ow**n	f**ou**nd
sp**oo**n	bl**oo**d	m**oo**n	r**oo**m
h**ar**d	d**ar**k	sc**are**	c**ar**d

■ Make up some sets of words of your own with an odd one out in each set. Use the back of this sheet.

Illustrations © Pete Smith/Beehive Illustration.

Dear helper
Objective: To investigate and classify words with the same sounds but different spellings.
Task: Look at the words and say them aloud with your child. Identify which is the odd word out in each set. Repeat the words several times if your child experiences difficulty in hearing the sounds. Then help your child to think of 'odd one out' sets.

Name	Date

How does it feel?

▪ You are going to guess what is in the feely bag.

▪ Ask your helper to help you write down your descriptions of what you feel in the bag.

Name of object	Descriptive words and phrases

Illustrations © Theresa Tibbetts/Beehive Illustration.

POETRY

Dear helper
Objective: To provide words and phrases that describe the unseen object in a feely bag.
Task: Provide a cloth or plastic bag in which to place an object. Your child should guess what it is and describe how it feels. Select three or four items such as a small teddy bear, a tube of toothpaste, an ice cube, ball of Plasticine. Place the items in the bag one at a time without your child seeing then, through discussion help your child to provide descriptions. Use the sheet above to write down the descriptions and what the object might be.

Name   Date

Create a poem

- Choose something you can see through the window at home.
  - ☐ It could be something large, like the lawn.
  - ☐ Or it could be something not so large, like a car.
  - ☐ Or it could be something quite small, like a stone.
- Follow the examples below to write your own poem.
- Think carefully about the best words to use in order to provide a word picture of what it is you have chosen.

	Poem 1	**Poem 2**
What is it? (a few words)	the tulip	my pedal car
Where is it? (a few words)	on a straight stalk	where I left it
What is it doing? (one word)	glowing	waiting.

- Write your poem here:

What is it?   _____

Where is it?   _____

What is it doing? _____

POETRY

Illustrations © Theresa Tibbetts/Beehive Illustration.

Dear helper
Objective: To compose a poem using carefully selected words to form a picture.
Task: Help your child with this task of composing a poem by talking about what can be seen through a window at home. Describe what can be seen, but focus on one thing to which your child is particularly drawn. Write down the things your child says about the subject, then help your child select the best words to use in the poem.

Name	Date

Be a poet

- Choose your favourite sweet, fruit or other food item.
- Write a poem using one word each to describe:
  - ☐ colour
  - ☐ sound
  - ☐ feels
  - ☐ smells
  - ☐ taste.

- Set it out like the example.

pink

squelching

sugary

freezing

strawberry

ice cream!

POETRY

Dear helper
Objective: To write a poem using a model.
Task: First, help your child choose a favourite food. Then talk about it with your child, perhaps jotting down some of the words used. Select the best words to fit each aspect of the poem and help your child to write these in the poem format. Read the poem with your child. Ask: *Does it read the way you want it to, or is there anything we need to change?*

Sort the rhymes

■ Sort these rhyming words by the spelling of their rhyming endings.

■ Place them correctly in the grid below.

bear	care	pear	bare	tear
snare	glare	hare	share	fare
stare	rare	flare	mare	swear

ear	are	other words

PHOTOCOPIABLE ■SCHOLASTIC
www.scholastic.co.uk

Illustrations © Theresa Tibbetts/Beehive Illustration.

CORE SKILLS

Sounds of the city

- Read the poem below.
- Underline the words in each verse that rhyme.
- Some of the words that rhyme have different spellings for the same sound.
Which words are these?

Scamper, scuttle,

Stop and stare,

Cities echoing sounds in the air.

Spring and stretch,

Stride and fuss,

Busy people rushing for a bus.

Circus in the city,

Dresses for the clown,

Stampeding horses make people frown.

Ice-cold drinks,

Sun beats down,

Sweltering people rush out of town.

Wendy Jolliffe

- Write a list of all the words that have the sound **s** in them on the back of this sheet.

Illustrations © Pete Smith/Beehive Illustration.

CORE SKILLS

Dear helper
Objective: To understand that the same sound can be represented by different spellings.
Task: Read the poem with your child once, then re-read it and ask your child to underline the rhyming words. Finally, help your child to find every word that contains the sound /s/. Talk about the different spellings of the sound ('s', 'se', 'ss', 'c', 'ce').

Name	Date

Time for...?

- Read the poem with your helper.
- Draw a line between the words that rhyme.

Christopher Sweet tucked his feet
Down to the bottom
Of the warm, warm sheet.
How many times did the church clock strike?
One, two, three, four, five,
Six, seven, EIGHT!

Caroline Tate is always late
She's only just running
Through the old school gate!
How many times
Did the school bell chime?
One, two, three, four, five,
Six, seven, eight, NINE!

Oliver Lee can't wait for tea,
school's nearly finished for him and me!
How many rings till we're all free?
One, two THREE!

Nicola Head won't go to bed.
'Chase her up the stairs then'
her mother said.
How many times
Did the clock strike then?
One, two, three, four, five,
Six, seven, eight, nine, TEN!

Marilyn Heap is fast asleep;
Listen at the door
But you won't hear a peep!
How many times
Did the church clock strike?
One, two, three, four, five,
Six, seven, eight, nine, ten,
      Eleven, twelve… MIDNIGHT!

Judith Nicholls

Poem © 1993, Judith Nicholls; illustrations © Theresa Tibbetts/Beehive Illustration.

Dear helper
Objective: To be able to predict rhyming words.
Task: Read the poem to your child, then read it again but pause before saying the rhyming words, such as *feet* and *sheet*. Do this several times. You could try covering the rhyming words with your finger and asking your child to say what they are.

Name   Date

Little Samantha's day

✂️

Little Samantha shouts "It's all gone!"

Little Samantha asleep with her bear.

Little Samantha puts jam on her bread.

Little Samantha eats sausages at one.

Little Samantha jumps out of her bed.

Little Samantha reads books in a chair.

◼ Put these sentences in the correct order to find out about little Samantha's day.

◼ First cut out the boxes.

◼ Then paste the sentences and pictures onto a separate sheet in the right order.

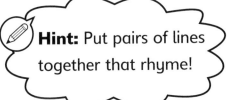

✏️ **Hint:** Put pairs of lines together that rhyme!

Illustrations © Theresa Tibbetts/Beehive Illustration.

Dear helper
Objective: To use rhyme and sense to re-order sentences into a sequenced and meaningful poem.
Task: Discuss the pictures and descriptions with your child and use the rhyme endings to help order the sentences correctly.

Name

Date

Ill in bed

● The poem below is jumbled up.

● Write it in the correct order so it makes sense.

Hint: Use the rhymes at the end of the lines to help you find the right order.

She gave me orange through a straw

One day when I was ill in bed

I couldn't draw, I could only look

And asked me if I'd like to draw

At pictures in my favourite book

My mother came and felt my head

● Write the poem here:

_____

_____

_____

_____

_____

Illustrations © Theresa Tibbetts/Beehive Illustration.

Dear helper
Objective: To re-order the sentences so that the poem makes sense.
Task: Help your child to read each line. Ask: *Which is the most likely line to begin the poem?* Point out the rhyme endings to help your child sort the sentences into the right order.

One to ten

■ Read these rhymes with a helper and try to learn them.
(You may know them already!)

One, two,   _____
Buckle my shoe.   _____
Three, four,   _____
Knock at the door.   _____
Five, six,   _____
Pick up sticks.   _____
Seven, eight,   _____
Lay them straight.   _____
Nine, ten,   _____
A big fat hen.   _____

One, two, three, four, five,   _____
Once I caught a fish alive.   _____
Six, seven, eight, nine, ten,   _____
Then I let it go again.   _____
Why did you let it go?   _____
Because it bit my finger so.   _____
Which finger did it bite?   _____
This little finger on my right.   _____

■ Write down pairs of rhyming words from the poems in the
space provided.
■ Can you add some more rhyming words of your own? Use the
back of this sheet.

Dear helper
Objective: To investigate words with the same sounds but different spellings.
Task: Read the poems and learn them together. Help your child to identify the rhyming words and to try
to think of other words that would rhyme with them.

CORE SKILLS

Time to rhyme

- Look at the words around the table.
- Now look at the words in the table.
- Write the words from around the table next to the word in the table that it rhymes with.

den   do

then   there   sly

laugh

wh or ph word	rhyming words
when	
why	
where	
who	
phone	
graph	
pheasant	
phase	

ten

groan   hair

try   days

dry   my

high   pleasant   alone   two

men   moan   fair

Dear helper
Objective: To read and spell words containing the letters 'wh' and 'ph' and to reinforce understanding of rhyme.
Task: Read the words aloud with your child and talk about the ways in which we usually pronounce 'wh' and 'ph'. Help your child to look at newspapers, books and so on to find more words that include 'wh' or 'ph'. Help your child to say the words correctly.

CORE SKILLS

Pick a pair

sand	help	mist	last
gulp	band	cast	pulp
mind	blast	fist	kind
spend	yelp	mend	rind
twist	past	find	list

◼ Cut out the word cards above.

◼ Jumble them up and lay them face down.

◼ Take turns to turn a pair over. If you turn over a pair that rhymes, keep it. The one with the most pairs at the end wins.

CORE SKILLS

Dear helper
Objective: To pick out rhyming words and to investigate their spellings.
Task: Help your child to investigate the spellings of the words, pointing out the word endings '-nd', '-lp' and '-st'.

Name   Date

Have you seen the crocodile?

- Look at the pictures.
- Fill in the missing words.

Have you seen the **crocodile**?   "No" said the **bee**.

Have you seen the _____ ?   "No" said the _____ .

Have you seen the _____ ?   "No" said the _____ .

Have you seen the _____ ?   "No" said the _____ .

Illustrations © Theresa Tibbetts/Beehive Illustration.

Dear helper
Objective: To substitute words in a patterned story.
Task: Help your child to fill in the missing words by looking at the pictures.

POETRY

Name _____   Date _____

The Bear's Just Had Twins!

📕 Fill in the missing rhyming words using this list:

day   **said**   **twins**   **eat**

see   **too**   **mood**

Illustrations © Theresa Tibbetts/Beehive Illustration.

POETRY

The Bear's Just Had Twins!

Skipping and hopping we went to the zoo

With mummy and daddy and baby came _____ .

We whistled and sang as we went on our way,

All looking forward to a beautiful _____ .

The sun in the sky shone bright overhead,

And, once at the gate, the zookeeper _____ ,

"Beware of the monkeys. They're throwing their food.

They woke up this morning in a mischievous _____ .

Please keep to the paths and put litter in bins.

Don't rattle the cages. The bear's just had _____ !"

"The bear's just had twins!" we all shouted with glee,

And briskly walked on so that we could _____

The two little bears all cuddly and sweet

Meowing like kittens wanting something to _____ .

Kathleen Taylor

Dear helper
Objective: To be able to predict the rhyming endings.
Task: Read the poem with expression for your child, pausing at the appropriate point in order that your child can supply the missing rhyming word.

Name	Date

Create an animal poem

◼ Choose a creature. It can be one you like very much, or one that you don't like.

◼ Write three things about it, using one word for each thing. Each word must begin with the same letter – like this:

What (or who) are they?	caterpillars
What do they do?	crawl
How do they do this?	creepily

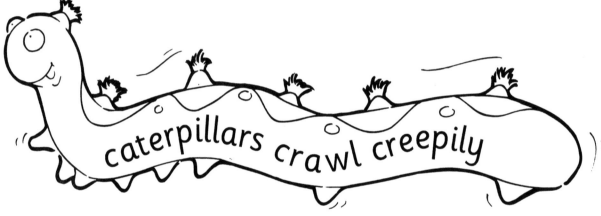

caterpillars crawl creepily

◼ Now you try:

What (or who) are they? _____

What do they do? _____

How do they do this? _____

Illustrations © Theresa Tibbetts/Beehive Illustration.

Dear helper
Objective: To compose a poem that has a poetic quality.
Task: Help your child by discussing the creature they chose, building a range of words to choose from and use when composing their own poem. If your child does this successfully, encourage them to write more than one poem.

PHOTOCOPIABLE ▮▮SCHOLASTIC
www.scholastic.co.uk

Capital letters hunt

◀ Read part of the story of *Slinky Malinki*, the cat who was a burglar!

◀ Put a ring around all the capital letters for names.

Slinky Malinki

One rascally night

between midnight and four,

Slinky Malinki

stole MORE than before.

Some pegs and a teddy bear

dressed up in lace,

a gardening glove

from Macafferty's place.

A tatty old sneaker,

a smelly old sock

and Jennifer Turkington's

pottery smock.

A squishy banana,

some glue and a pen,

a cushion from

Oliver Tulliver's den.

Poem © 1991, Lynley Dodd; Illustrations © Theresa Tibbetts/Beehive Illustration.

CORE SKILLS

Dear helper
Objective: To identify capital letters for names.
Task: Read the above extract from *Slinky Malinki* by Lynley Dodd with your child. Talk about capital letters and say that one of the uses for capital letters is for people's names. Remind your child how to begin to write their own name. Give your child a pen or pencil and ask them to put a ring round every capital letter for someone's name. You can then help to write a list of all the names mentioned above. Explain that the word *more* is in capitals just to make it stand out.

Slinky Malinki

- Read the story with your helper.
- Cut out the words and find them in the story.

Slinky Malinki
was blacker than black,
a stalking and lurking
adventurous cat.
He had bright yellow eyes,
a warbling wail
And a kink at the end
of his very long tail.
He was cheeky and cheerful,
friendly and fun,
he'd chase after leaves
and he'd roll in the sun.
But at night he was wicked
And fiendish and sly.
Through moonlight and shadow
He'd prowl and he'd pry.
He crept over fences,
He leaped over walls,
He poked into corners
And sneaked into halls.
What was he up to?
At night, to be brief,
Slinky Malinki
Turned into a
THIEF.

| cat |
| eyes |
| sun |
| night |
| fences |
| walls |
| leaves |
| corners |
| tail |
| halls |
| thief |
| shadow |

Poem © 1991, Lynley Dodd; illustrations © Theresa Tibbetts/Beehive Illustration.

CORE SKILLS

Dear helper
Objective: To match spoken to printed words.
Task: Read the extract from the story *Slinky Malinki* by Lynley Dodd to your child. Talk about who Slinky Malinki is and what he's like. Now cut out the words above and spread them out. Read them to your child. Now re-read the extract, pointing to the words as you do so, and look for one word that you have cut out at a time. You might turn the words over when you have found them, or put them in a pile. You could also make up more sentences using these words.

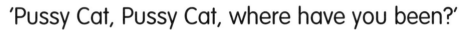

Pussy Cat, Pussy Cat

◾ Read the poem and listen for the long vowel sounds **ee** (as in **been**) and **ai** (as in **train**).

◾ Make two collections, one of the words you find with the sound **ee** in them, and another for words with the sound **ai** in them.

◾ Sort them by their different spellings and put them in the grids.

'Pussy Cat, Pussy Cat, where have you been?'

'I've been on a train to see the Queen.'

'Pussy Cat, Pussy Cat, what did she say?'

'Pleased to meet you, but you can't stay all day.'

'Pussy Cat, Pussy Cat, did you think she was mean?'

'Oh no! She was busy, after all she's the Queen.'

CORE SKILLS

Illustrations © Theresa Tibbetts/Beehive Illustration.

ee	
e	
ea	
ai	
ay	

Dear helper

Objective: To identify the long vowel sounds by their sound and learn their different spelling patterns.

Task: Help your child to read the poem. It is best to track one sound at a time, so, first of all, help your child to listen and pick out all the /ee/ sounds, writing them in the grid. Then, do the same for the /ai/ sounds. You may wish to continue this activity using other texts and adding to the number of spelling patterns in the grids.

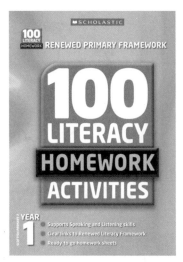

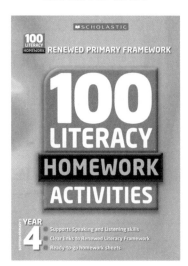

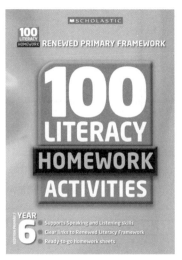